Retirement Redefined

A Comprehensive Planning Guide to a Fun and Fulfilling Retirement

Mary Rose

losses, direct or indirect, that are incurred as a result of the use of the information contained within this document, including, but not limited to, errors, omissions, or inaccuracies.

Table of Contents

Introduction

Are you approaching retirement and feeling unsure about how to make the most of your golden years? This comprehensive guide offers in-depth and practical ideas for redefining retirement and creating a fulfilling post-work lifestyle. The time to think about it is now! Retirees are living longer, and with a fluid financial landscape and a new definition of quality of life, you're left with a longer and more exciting retirement future.

This changing retirement landscape can leave you puzzled, and with a lot more to think about than you anticipated. Enter *Retirement Redefined*, your guide to successful retirement planning!

From where you'll live to how you can stay healthier for longer, this book covers it all. Challenge traditional notions of retirement and embrace personal growth, learning, and exploration. Discover actionable advice for navigating retirement challenges, building a strong social network, staying active and healthy, traveling, and finding purpose and fulfillment. Whether you're a baby boomer or a member of Generation X, this ultimate guide empowers you to create a uniquely fulfilling retirement lifestyle.

As a newly retired single woman, former teacher, mother, and nana, I wanted to share the knowledge I gained through experience. On my own journey, I have gained much insight into the many facets of the retirement journey. Approach this significant life change with confidence, creativity, and purpose.

With the help of this book, you can take the first steps on your journey to discover the profound importance of planning for your retirement. You will explore how this transformative process can shape your retiree life into a truly fulfilling and secure adventure. Planning is the key to your financial security—setting achievable goals and carefully assessing your income, savings, expenses, investments, and debts.

In *Retirement Redefined*, you will explore the profound significance of financial security in retirement. Through self-reflection, you'll see how planning empowers you to make informed decisions about budgeting, debt management, and maximizing your income streams. This book provides practical tips and strategies to safeguard your financial well-being throughout your retirement.

We'll delve into the need for goals based on your unique circumstances, desired lifestyle, and health care needs. With inflation boosting costs of living, many retirees feel less stable and comfortable with the plans they chose. Because of this, we will also explore evaluating income streams including pensions, Social Security benefits, and investment returns to support your retirement lifestyle. Additionally, we'll offer guidance on managing debt and crafting a budget that allows you to live within your means while embracing joyful activities and experiences.

Retirement planning is not just about finances; it's a journey of self-discovery. In the upcoming chapters, you'll discover the significance of setting goals. This book will be your trusted companion, helping you envision your ideal lifestyle and identify specific milestones. By doing this, you'll chart a clear path toward the retirement of your dreams.

Effective resource allocation is crucial in retirement planning. By managing your financial assets thoughtfully, you can create a comfortable and fulfilling retirement. In Chapter 1, we'll explore the importance of planning as well as manage savings and pensions. These strategies will help you optimize your resources and ensure a satisfying retirement.

Retirement planning can be a challenging endeavor for many seniors as they navigate the complexities of this significant life transition. The uncertainties that come with leaving the workforce and entering a new phase of life can be overwhelming. However, with knowledge and preparation—and perhaps some help from a professional—these challenges can be made easier, allowing seniors to approach retirement with confidence and peace of mind.

In this book, we will prepare for transitions and provide you with the tools and insights to navigate them with ease. When you retire, you bid farewell to your career, and you begin this new chapter in life. By understanding the various aspects of retirement planning, from financial considerations to lifestyle adjustments, you can proactively prepare yourself for the road ahead.

We will explore the concepts of phased retirement and part-time work. We will discuss the possibility of gradually transitioning into retirement, allowing you to maintain a sense of purpose, engagement, and financial stability. By considering these options, you may be able to ease the transition from full-time work to a more flexible and fulfilling lifestyle.

Finding purpose in retirement is another essential aspect we will explore. Retirement is about leisure, and it's about discovering new passions, engaging in meaningful activities, and making a positive impact in your community. We will guide you in uncovering your unique interests and talents, and help you find purpose and fulfillment in this new lifestyle. Through the art of preparation, you can embark on an exhilarating journey filled with endless possibilities.

By equipping yourself with knowledge, understanding the challenges that may arise, and proactively planning for those challenges, you can navigate the complexities of retirement with confidence and grace. This book will serve as your trusted companion, providing you with the guidance, insights, and practical advice you need to make informed decisions and embrace the exciting path that lies ahead. As you explore the intricacies of retirement planning, you will gain the skills to create a retirement lifestyle that is uniquely fulfilling and meaningful to you. With knowledge, preparation, and a sense of adventure, you can confidently step into retirement ready to embrace the extraordinary possibilities that it has to offer.

Imagine the incredible tapestry of possibilities that lies before you! Delve into personal fulfillment and joy, where every decision is a brushstroke on the canvas of your dreams. In the forthcoming chapters, you'll reflect on the significance of lifestyle considerations in retirement planning. You'll explore housing choices, travel plans, hobbies, and social activities. By crafting a retirement lifestyle aligned with your passions and aspirations, you can fashion a masterpiece of contentment and bliss.

Retirement planning goes beyond the immediate future. It involves taking care of your long-term needs and considering end-of-life matters. In *Retirement Redefined*, you'll consider the importance of long-term care and end-of-life planning. You'll learn about planning for future health care, housing, expenses, and estate planning. By addressing these aspects now, you can have peace of mind and ensure your wishes are fulfilled. Prepare yourself to discover the profound importance of nurturing your health and well-being throughout retirement. This book will help you remain physically vibrant, mentally agile, and emotionally content. We'll identify potential hurdles and provide a holistic guide to getting over them.

As you progress through the book, I recommend that you reflect deeply on your aspirations and goals for retirement. Envision the life you want and think about how planning can help you achieve that vision. Retirement is a beginning, an opportunity to explore your passions and create a fulfilling life.

Whether you're just starting or already immersed in retirement planning, this book is an invaluable resource. The insights, strategies, and ideas shared in these pages will empower you to make informed decisions and forge a retirement that brings fulfillment and security. Are you prepared to embark on this incredible journey? Let's get started!

Chapter 1:

Planning for a Purposeful

Retirement

Welcome to your retirement planning manual! Congratulations, as you've achieved one of the biggest milestones in life. You've had a successful career, and now it's time to reap the rewards! Retirement has evolved a lot in recent decades, which may surprise you now that you approach the end of your career. In the past, retirement meant bidding farewell to work and settling into a life of relaxation and leisure. But now, you have more options available than ever!

The process of retirement planning that you're about to embark upon may feel laborious, but it will help you have a happier retirement and possibly improve your longevity. While most of us are blessed with longer lives, those additional years pose a need for greater retirement savings and better retirement planning. Chapter 1 will be dedicated to a better understanding of retirement and retirement planning.

Understanding Retirement

Retirement is an incredible journey, a transition from the hustle and bustle of work to a life of leisure and pursuing your passions. It's like turning the page to a brand new chapter, filled with endless possibilities and exciting adventures. But let's take a moment to reflect on what retirement truly means. You've worked hard throughout your career, dedicating your time and energy to building a secure future. Along the way, you've diligently saved a portion of your earnings and made wise investments, all with the goal of creating a comfortable retirement. Now, as you embark on this new phase of life, it's time to put those savings to good use.

But here's the thing: retirement isn't just about kicking back and relaxing (although that's definitely an option—and a perk!). Retirement means the opportunity to grow, explore, and chase your dreams. It's about finding new passions, discovering hidden talents, and nurturing your well-being.

To make the most of this exciting journey, it's crucial to plan ahead. By considering important factors like your income, health, lifestyle, investments, and estate planning, you can ensure a smoother transition into retirement. Planning allows you to have a clear vision of how you want your retirement to look, and helps you adapt to any unexpected twists and turns along the way.

When you plan, you set yourself up for a secure and joyful retirement. You have peace of mind knowing your financial needs, health, and dreams are satisfied. Let's embark on this adventure with a solid plan and some excitement. Your retirement awaits!

It Is... All About You!

You admirably have dedicated your life to contributing to your community and supporting your family and friends. Now is the time to enjoy the fruits of your labor and create the lifestyle you deserve. While some retirees choose to continue supporting loved ones, the decision is yours. This book does not advocate for a specific choice or lifestyle. Instead, it suggests that you make intentional decisions about your future. With this in mind, consider embracing a more self-indulgent mindset to reward yourself for your hard work. However, embracing the freedoms and rewards of retirement requires thoughtful balancing of tasks and to-dos, as well as weighing your income against your spending needs. In the following sections, you will gain more insight into the most important aspects to consider in this regard.

Time to Fulfill Your Dreams!

Retirement offers the opportunity to pursue dreams and passions while enjoying an active lifestyle. It allows you to prioritize personal fulfillment and engage in activities that may have been put aside. Additionally, with ample time, you can embrace hobbies, interests, and passions that bring you joy. Remember that patience, support, and encouragement can make a difference on this journey. As a retiree, you have the chance to explore new horizons and embark on exciting adventures. You can travel to new destinations, immersing yourself in different cultures and fulfilling your dreams. Retirement opens doors to endless possibilities.

Retirement is not about slowing down; it's about maintaining an active lifestyle. You can participate in physical activities to stay energized and engaged. Participating in regular exercise will keep your body strong and healthy. Joining social events will help you connect with like-minded people. Additionally, you can volunteer for causes you care about to make a positive impact.

Retirement is a time for learning and growth. You can enroll in courses and workshops, or pursue online education to expand your knowledge and acquire new skills. Embrace lifelong learning and discover new passions. Retirement offers endless opportunities for personal growth, including giving back to your community through volunteering, mentoring, and community service projects. Contribute to society and find purpose and fun in your golden years.

An extended retirement period allows you to prioritize your physical, mental, and emotional well-being. Take the time to indulge in self-care activities that bring you fun and fulfillment. Embrace mindfulness practices to find inner peace and tranquility. Maintain a healthy lifestyle that nourishes your body and your mind. This is your time to shine and embrace a lighthearted, warm, uplifting, and optimistic approach to life!

Emotional and Psychological Preparation

Emotional and psychological preparation is a crucial part of your retirement planning journey. Prepare yourself to make the adjustments that accompany the retirement transition. Let's explore why this preparation is so important and discover effective ways to address it.

Adjusting to New Routines and Finding Purpose

Retirement brings a significant change to your daily schedule. After years of following a work routine, you'll have more free time and fewer obligations This new chapter in your life can be both exciting and challenging. However, fear not! You have the opportunity to embrace it with open arms.

Start by exploring new hobbies, activities, and routines that will bring you fun and fulfillment during retirement. Get ready to embark on this wonderful journey of self-discovery and endless possibilities! Although retirement may sometimes leave you feeling like you've lost your sense of identity and purpose, you have nothing to fear.

Take a moment to reflect on your values, interests, and passions. Use this time to embark on a journey of self-discovery and find new sources of purpose and meaning in your retirement years. You can volunteer your time, pursue creative projects that ignite your soul, keep learning and expanding your horizons, or get involved in your community. By exploring these new avenues, you'll not only find a renewed sense of fulfillment, but also experience deep satisfaction in your post-work life. Embrace this exciting chapter with open arms and let your true passions guide you to a life filled with fun and purpose!

Transition With Connectivity and Wellness

If you're worried about transitioning from full-time work to complete retirement, some alternatives may suit you better. Have you thought about phased retirement or part-time work? Instead of abruptly stopping work, you can gradually reduce your hours, or take on a different role within your organization. Opting for part-time work allows you to stay engaged, maintain social connections, and supplement your retirement income. These options are worth exploring to find the perfect balance for you. Remember, staying connected and having a support network is crucial as you enter retirement.

Retirement can sometimes lead to feelings of isolation because you have fewer daily interactions. However, you can take the initiative to build and maintain social connections. Join clubs, organizations, or community groups that interest you, and stay in touch with friends, family, and colleagues. By building a strong support system, you'll experience emotional well-being and a deep sense of belonging throughout your retirement journey.

To have a truly fulfilling retirement experience, prioritize self-care and well-being. Take time to focus on your personal health, relaxation, and stress reduction. Incorporate activities like exercise, meditation, hobbies, and self-reflection into your daily routine. By taking care of your emotional and physical well-being, you'll set yourself up for a retirement filled with fun and contentment. Preparing for retirement can be complex, but you're not alone in this journey. Seeking professional guidance from retirement coaches, therapists, or counselors who specialize in retirement transitions can be incredibly helpful. They provide valuable support, offering guidance, tools, and strategies to navigate the emotional and psychological aspects of retirement effectively.

Whether you use a professional or do it on your own, several important steps can make the journey smoother. Retirees can adapt to new routines and discover a sense of purpose in their post-work life. Additionally, exploring options like phased retirement or part-time work can provide a gradual shift into retirement, aligning with their preferences. Building strong social connections is essential for staying engaged and connected with others. Prioritizing self-care, both physically and mentally, is vital for overall well-being.

Setting Retirement Goals

Retirement goals revolve around figuring out what you want to accomplish during your golden years. They're all about embracing your wildest dreams and moving toward those incredible milestones. So, let's delve into why setting retirement goals can improve your life, and explore how you can make them a reality. Get ready for an exciting journey!

Picture Your Dream Life

Retirement goals enable you to envision a vibrant and fulfilling post-work life. Imagine the lifestyle you desire, the activities that bring you joy, and the experiences you've always wanted. With a clear vision, you can craft a retirement plan that aligns perfectly with your values and aspirations. Moreover, retirement presents an incredible opportunity to focus on what truly brings you fun and fulfillment.

First and foremost, prioritize your passions and pursue activities that light up your soul. Whether it's exploring new hobbies, embarking on personal growth journeys, or finding ways to give back to your community, the possibilities are endless. By setting goals and making your aspirations a priority, you'll ensure that your retirement years are filled with purpose and fulfillment. Let's make every moment count!

Money Matters

Retirement goals are essential for estimating your financial needs. When you envision the lifestyle you desire and the activities you plan to pursue, you can determine the amount of money you'll need to make it all a reality. This estimation becomes your compass for financial planning, allowing you to set achievable savings and investment targets. By setting clear retirement goals, you empower yourself to create the future you've always wanted.

Aim for the Stars

Retirement goals provide you with clear objectives. They offer a sense of purpose and direction as you enter your golden years. Think about anything you may want! Whether you dream of exploring exotic destinations, embarking on a new business venture, dedicating your time to a cause close to your heart, or simply cherishing precious moments with your loved ones, having well-defined goals keeps you motivated and focused on what truly matters.

Embrace Change

Setting retirement goals is an ongoing process. As you journey through retirement, your goals may evolve or change completely. You should regularly review and adjust your goals to reflect your changing circumstances, interests, and priorities. By doing so, you can stay flexible and seize new opportunities that come your way. So, keep dreaming, exploring, and embracing the exciting possibilities that retirement has to offer!

Travel Time

Retirement brings you the wonderful freedom to travel more. So, dive into your travel aspirations and create a fantastic plan to explore new destinations or revisit your all-time favorite places. Just imagine the incredible travel experiences you can have, now that you don't have to get back to your job! Take a moment to think about what kind of adventures you desire, your budget, any health considerations, and the specific goals you have in mind. By planning your travel options, you can seamlessly incorporate enriching experiences into your retirement lifestyle. It's time to embark on unforgettable journeys and make the most of your well-deserved retirement!

Hobby Heaven

Retirement presents you with the perfect opportunity to embrace those hobbies and interests you may have neglected. Consider engaging in activities that bring you pure joy, such as painting, gardening, music, or sports. You can also explore various clubs or groups that align with your interests. By incorporating your hobbies into your retirement lifestyle, you not only find purpose and personal growth but also foster meaningful social connections. Plan to indulge in what truly brings you happiness!

Social Butterfly

Maintaining an active social life is crucial for your overall well-being during retirement. You can enhance your retirement experience by considering social activities that align with your interests and values. Join community organizations, volunteer, participate in fitness classes, or attend social events. Set a goal of building and nurturing social connections, and you'll create a vibrant and fulfilling retirement.

Your desired lifestyle may change over time, so stay open to new opportunities and be willing to adapt your plans. As you enter retirement, you have the freedom to explore different options that align with your preferences and changing interests. Embrace the exciting possibilities that lie ahead and embrace the fun of discovering new paths to happiness. Remember, retirement is a time to live life to the fullest and create a fulfilling and vibrant future for yourself.

In a nutshell, retirement planning involves considering your lifestyle options. By exploring what you truly desire, you can create a retirement that perfectly aligns with your values, interests, and aspirations. Keep the financial side in mind, but also stay flexible and open to new opportunities. Embrace all the amazing possibilities that retirement brings and enjoy the journey ahead!

Future Health Care Needs

As you approach your golden years, consider various aspects of your well-being. Take a moment to reflect on potential medical expenses, ensure you have adequate health insurance coverage, and explore long-term care options. Assess your health status, take into account your family's medical history, and address any specific concerns you may have. Research health care options such as long-term care insurance, Medicare, and Medicaid to discover coverage and resources tailored to your needs.

Taking proactive steps now can provide peace of mind and ensure a bright and secure future. Consider the possibility that you may need assistance with your daily activities or a change in your living situation. You can explore various long-term care options such as assisted living facilities, nursing homes, or in-home care services. Take the time to learn about the costs and financing options available to you for these potential expenses. Additionally, think about any necessary housing changes that may be needed to accommodate your evolving needs. Remember, planning ahead can help ensure a smooth transition and provide you with peace of mind.

You can start by communicating your medical treatment preferences and designating someone to make health care decisions on your behalf if needed. Have these conversations with your loved ones and document your directives for easy access during emergencies. By doing so, you ensure that your wishes are known and can be followed, providing you with peace of mind.

Regular Review and Updates

To keep your health care plans up to date, make a habit of regularly reviewing and adjusting them as needed. Remember, life is full of unexpected twists and turns, so stay proactive and ensure that your plans align with your wishes and circumstances. By staying on top of things, you can embrace any changes that come your way with confidence, and make the most out of every opportunity that comes knocking on your door.

Along with health care plans, you also need to make a regular habit of reviewing and adjusting your financial plan. Doing so will enable you to adapt to the ever-changing circumstances and market conditions. By skillfully allocating your resources, you'll not only optimize your financial assets but also embrace a future that is secure, abundant, and deeply fulfilling.

Long-term planning is incredibly important while preparing for your retirement. Look ahead to ensure that you're well-prepared for various aspects of your future. And of course, you can't overlook the significance of end-of-life planning. This includes essential matters such as estate planning, wills, trusts, health care directives, and personal family affairs. From health care needs to potential changes in housing and expenses, you have a lot to consider.

Remember, when it comes to long-term planning, it's important to be prepared and ensure that your wishes are respected. If you ever need guidance, don't hesitate to reach out to professionals who can assist you in navigating the process and ensuring that your plans are comprehensive and legally sound.

Ultimately, this chapter showed you how important it is to set goals and plan your retirement well. A longer time frame, for all its blessings, also means a longer retirement, more need for savings, and better use of the money and assets that you already have. Planning makes that successful.

Chapter 2:

Financial Considerations

As you slowly dip your toes into retirement planning, you would be wise to start with the most difficult task: finances. Dealing with finances is stressful for everyone. No matter how organized you think you are, when you begin putting everything into place before retiring, there's always more work than anticipated.

In this chapter, you will learn how to assess your finances and make important decisions concerning your expenses, assets, and needs. This will help you figure out how you're doing financially, and whether or not you might need some extra income or a professional advisor's help.

Assess Your Financial Situation

Assessing your financial situation for retirement doesn't have to be daunting. Take a moment to examine your income, savings, investments, and debts. By understanding these aspects, a clearer picture of your financial health will emerge. To calculate your net worth, think of it as figuring out the difference between your assets (property, investments, savings) and your liabilities (debts and loans). This will give you a better idea of your current financial standing and determine how much you can invest or save for retirement.

First, review your cash flow and your income sources and expenses to see how much money is coming in and how much is going out each month. This will help you find areas where you can cut back on expenses or boost your income. By thoroughly assessing your financial situation, you'll have a solid foundation for creating a retirement plan that matches your dreams and goals. You'll be able to make informed decisions about how much to save and how to manage your debts wisely. Remember, the more thorough your assessment, the better prepared you'll be for a financially secure retirement! Getting started early will make retirement planning a breeze! Here are some ideas for you to consider.

Income Sources

Your employer's pension plan is a treasure chest waiting to be opened for your retirement. Uncover all the details of your plan, such as when you can begin reaping its benefits and how they might evolve based on your years of service or your age. It's time to explore the exciting possibilities that you have!

Social Security

Ah, the sweet sound of Social Security benefits! It's like a cozy blanket of income during retirement. Explore the eligibility requirements and calculate your benefits based on your earnings history. Also, think about the best time to claim your benefits for maximum enjoyment.

Investments and Savings

When considering financial planning, take a moment to reflect on a few important considerations. First, approach your investments carefully and diversify across various assets to minimize risk. Take into account your personal risk tolerance and prioritize investments that offer stability and generate income. Additionally, be mindful of the impact of inflation on your savings. To safeguard against rising prices, consider investing in assets that can keep pace with inflation. Moreover, you should establish an emergency fund to handle unforeseen expenses, and prioritize paying off high-interest debt before entering retirement. Finally, don't overlook the significance of factoring in health care costs and exploring options such as insurance.

Part-Time Work

Retirement doesn't mean you have to hang up your hat completely! You can still add some extra sparkle to your bank account by working part-time. Explore opportunities that match your interests and skills, whether it's consulting, freelancing, or pursuing a passion project. It's all about finding the perfect blend of income sources to create a retirement symphony that's stable and sustainable. And hey, remember to tap into the wisdom of a financial advisor who can guide you through this exciting journey based on your unique circumstances and goals.

Determine Retirement Expenses

To make planning for your retirement more efficient, figure out which costs you know you'll need to include in your budget. Consider these factors when estimating your expenses.

Home Sweet Home

Think about your housing needs during retirement. Consider whether you will own your home outright or have mortgage or rent payments. Don't forget to take into account property taxes, insurance, maintenance, and any potential downsizing or modifications that may be necessary. Plan ahead and make sure your housing situation aligns with your retirement goals. By taking these factors into consideration, you can ensure a comfortable and worry-free living arrangement as you enjoy your golden years.

Health Is Wealth

As you age, health care costs have a tendency to increase. Estimate your expenses for various health care needs, such as insurance premiums, deductibles, co-pays, prescription medications, and potential long-term care. Look into Medicare options and supplemental insurance plans to fully understand the coverage and costs that are included. By doing so, you can better prepare for your future needs and ensure that you have the necessary supports in place.

Daily Delights

Time to consider your day-to-day expenses. Think about groceries, utilities, transportation, and household supplies. Are there any changes in your spending habits or lifestyle choices that might affect these expenses during retirement? Plan ahead and make adjustments if needed. Remember, retirement is a new chapter in your life, and with a little foresight, you can ensure that your day-to-day expenses are manageable and won't cause any unnecessary stress.

Adventure Awaits

If you're dreaming of travel in retirement, consider the various costs involved. Before you set off on your grand adventures, consider the financial aspects and incorporate them into your budget and plan. Travel costs can vary depending on the destinations, modes of transportation, accommodations, and activities you choose.

Do your research and estimate the expenses involved in your desired travel experiences. This includes not only the obvious costs like flights and hotels, but also factors like meals, transportation within the destination, entrance fees to attractions, and any additional activities or excursions you wish to indulge in.

First, there's transportation to think about. Whether you're flying, taking a train, or embarking on a road trip, you can budget for these expenses. Next, think about accommodations. Finding comfortable and affordable places to stay helps you enjoy your travels.

Then, there's the matter of meals. Exploring new cuisines and dining out can be a delightful part of your adventures. Lastly, don't forget about activities. From sightseeing to trying new experiences, there's so much to do and see. So as you plan your retirement travels, think about how often you'd like to go and which destinations are on your bucket list.

By carefully considering these costs and incorporating them into your retirement budget, you can ensure that your travel adventures align with your financial goals and resources. This will allow you to enjoy your journeys without worrying about overspending or compromising your financial security.

Fun and Fulfillment

During retirement, don't forget about your hobbies, memberships, and commitments. You might have expenses related to various activities that bring you ease and fulfillment. In addition to travel, retirement is also a wonderful time to explore those interests and hobbies—as long as you budget for them.

Consider joining clubs, taking classes, or volunteering for causes that resonate with you. These activities can add excitement, purpose, and a sense of fulfillment to your retirement years. Some of them may have costs involved. Embrace the opportunity to nurture existing passions and discover new ones, but don't let them catch you financially off-guard.

With careful financial planning and a focus on personal interests, your retirement years can be filled with joy, fulfillment, and the freedom to pursue your dreams. Remember to be realistic when estimating your retirement expenses. Take into account factors like inflation and potential unforeseen costs such as home repairs or emergencies. Assess your current spending habits and adjust them to align with your retirement goals. By estimating your retirement expenses, you can create a solid financial plan. Consulting with a financial advisor can give you some amazing insights and assist you in making informed decisions about your retirement budget. You've totally got this!

Consider the Financial Implications of Housing

When considering housing, think about how your choices can affect your finances. As a senior or retiree, finding the perfect housing option can greatly impact your financial well-being. So research the different housing options that are available to you and how they can align with your financial plans and desired lifestyle. Take a moment to explore these housing options and the potential financial implications. Here are a few factors worth considering.

Embrace Downsizing

Picture this: a smaller home or apartment that not only brings financial benefits but also lightens your load. Say goodbye to hefty mortgage payments, property taxes, and maintenance expenses. Plus, downsizing can unlock the equity you've built up, and that can be a game-changer for your retirement savings or other financial goals.

Discover New Horizons

Have you considered the excitement of moving to a new area? It's like embarking on a thrilling adventure! You'll be delighted to discover that some places offer a lower cost of living, allowing your retirement savings to stretch even farther. You never know, your dream retirement spot might be just around the corner!

Explore Exciting Alternatives

Retirement is your time to exercise financial freedoms, make wise decisions, and take a calculated risk or two. Why not explore housing options that match your lifestyle? Think about downsizing to a cozy condominium or townhouse, or even joining a vibrant retirement community or assisted living facility. Have you ever considered co-housing with like-minded individuals? It's like having a built-in support system and lifelong friends!

Financial Wizardry

Before making any housing decisions, talk numbers. Crunch those financial figures and see the potential savings or costs of downsizing or relocating. Take into account property values, rental rates, homeowners association fees, and any sneaky tax implications. Align these choices with your retirement budget and financial goals. And if you need some expert guidance, don't hesitate to consult a financial advisor. With a bit more thoughtful planning, you can create a retirement plan that's as unique as you are!

Consider Health and Long-Term Care Costs

When planning for retirement, keep your health and potential long-term care needs in mind. These important points are worth a look.

Taking Care of Your Health

As you age, health care expenses have a way of sneaking up on you. So be sure to estimate your health care needs and expenses. This includes considering insurance premiums, deductibles, co-pays, and prescription medications. Make sure to explore Medicare options and supplemental insurance plans to fully understand what they cover and how much they cost. By being proactive and informed, you can better prepare for your health care journey and ensure peace of mind in your golden years.

Long-Term Care

You may find yourself in need of a little extra assistance with your daily activities such as bathing, dressing, and eating. That's when long-term care becomes invaluable. It's definitely worth exploring the various long-term care insurance options available to you. These options can help alleviate the financial burden associated with receiving care in a nursing home, assisted living facility, or even in the comfort of your own home.

Consider the costs linked to various insurance options when choosing between different insurance plans. These would include premiums, deductibles, and potential out-of-pocket expenses. Understand how these expenses align with your overall retirement budget and financial plan. After all, it's your peace of mind and financial well-being we're talking about here!

It's important to fully comprehend what these policies cover and any potential limitations they may have. But rest assured, with the right long-term care plan, you can embrace each day with peace of mind and the freedom to live life to the fullest!

Get Some Professional TLC

Consider reaching out to a financial advisor or retirement planning specialist. They can offer guidance and expertise, and help you navigate any tricky financial decisions. They can also help you create a comprehensive retirement plan that's tailored to your specific goals and circumstances. Remember, retirement planning is an ongoing adventure. By regularly reviewing and adjusting your retirement plan, you can stay on track and make the necessary changes to ensure a financially secure retirement.

You may want to consider finding a retirement planning professional who can help you maximize your earnings and income. Consider using them for the following:

- Tailored Retirement Plan: Experts will create a retirement plan just for you. They'll consider your unique needs and goals to develop a plan that fits like a glove.

- Investment Magic: Let the professionals evaluate investment options and guide you toward the best choices. They'll make sure your investments are as solid as a rock.

- Income Wizardry: Need help generating income during retirement? The financial advisor will work their magic to optimize your income sources and make sure your retirement years are golden.

- Tax Tricks: These pros know all the tax secrets! They'll help you navigate the tax maze and minimize your tax liability. It's like having a personal tax wizard by your side.

- Plan Adjustments: Life is full of surprises, but don't worry! The financial advisor will regularly review and adjust your retirement plan. They'll keep you on track and alert you to new opportunities.

When choosing an advisor, look for someone with qualifications, experience, and a stellar reputation. You want a superhero who's certified and has your best interests at heart. Remember, seeking professional advice is like having a trusty sidekick on your retirement journey. It's the key to creating a solid retirement plan that will make you feel like a superhero yourself!

In this chapter, you learned about the various ways to review your finances and make them more stable. This will help you have a smoother retirement with more money at your disposal. Now that you've dealt with finances, it's time to think about whether you want to add to what you already have. In the next chapter, you'll see how continuing to work in retirement can benefit your financial and psychological health.

Chapter 3:

Continuing to Earn

You'll be thrilled to discover that countless retirees just like yourself are wholeheartedly embracing the concept of staying vibrant and engaged during their golden years. This chapter is all about the incredible opportunities that lie ahead for you as a retiree who desires to keep earning on your own unique terms. We'll look into the financial perks, the transition from full-time work, the chance to pursue your passions and interests, and the flexibility of remote work and the gig economy. The possibilities for ongoing education and training are endless, and could add power to the remarkable social and emotional benefits that accompany working at a job you love on a schedule you determine.

Financial Benefits

Working in some capacity during retirement can bring you significant financial benefits. You can supplement your retirement income, reduce your reliance on savings, and boost your financial security. By earning extra income, you can maintain a comfortable lifestyle, handle unexpected expenses, and even give your retirement savings a chance to grow over time. It's a win-win situation for you!

How do you decide whether continuing to work, and at what capacity, is wise? Perhaps the best way to decide is to weigh the benefits against any downsides. As with everything else, careful planning helps. Here are some things that you should consider:

Do You Need to Work?

Calculate your financial situation. If you have savings and investments that can support your retirement lifestyle, then working will be more for the sake of fulfillment rather than financial benefit. To make this decision, think about your living expenses, health care costs, and any outstanding debts and other commitments.

Will Working Make You Happy?

Reflect on whether continuing to work would bring you joy, a sense of purpose, and fulfillment. Some people enjoy pursuing part-time or volunteer work that aligns with their interests and passions. You may want to give it a try.

Can You Strike a Balance?

Consider how continuing to work will impact your retirement work-life balance. Do you want more free time, or would you prefer to stay engaged in work? Some retirees find keeping up with their productive routines refreshing, to some degree.

Is Your Health a Concern?

Physical or mental health concerns or any chronic illness you may have might require more time for self-care. In that case, retiring fully might be the best option. On the other hand, some people find that staying active through work positively impacts their well-being.

Where's Your Social Network?

Consider the social aspect of work. If your job provides a strong sense of community and social interaction, you may want to continue working to maintain those connections.

Does It Have to Be All or Nothing?

If you're unsure about retiring completely, consider a phased retirement approach. This could involve reducing your work hours gradually or exploring flexible work arrangements.

Ultimately, the decision on whether to continue working will depend on your personal circumstances, goals, and priorities. As mentioned earlier, you can weigh your options with a financial advisor, career counselor, or a trusted family member or friend.

You have various options as you transition from full-time work. Embracing part-time employment or flexible work arrangements enables you to maintain a harmonious work-life balance while enjoying the benefits of retirement. Consider consulting, freelancing, contracting, mentoring, or even starting your own small business. These avenues empower you to leverage your expertise and experience on your own terms, opening up a world of possibilities.

Pursue Passions, Hobbies, and Interests

Retirees today are embracing a new trend: pursuing jobs and hobbies that bring fun, fulfillment, and income. This shift in mindset is transforming the retirement landscape for several reasons. One main reason is the desire for continued engagement and purpose. Traditional notions of retirement no longer resonate with retirees' aspirations. You seek opportunities to stay active, contribute to society, and maintain productivity. By pursuing income-generating activities, retirees can achieve these goals simultaneously.

The availability of flexible work options and the rise of the gig economy have also contributed to the popularity of income-generating activities during retirement. You now have access to part-time, freelance, and remote work opportunities that didn't exist in the past. This flexibility allows you to strike a balance between freedom and meaningful work. The digital age has further opened up possibilities for retirees to monetize your skills, knowledge, and passions. You can use online platforms and marketplaces to offer your expertise, services, and products to people around the globe.

Financial considerations also play a role in the popularity of income-generating activities during retirement. With increasing life expectancies and rising costs of living, retirees seek ways to supplement retirement savings and ensure financial security. By generating income through jobs and hobbies, you can enjoy a comfortable lifestyle, pursue interests, and have the freedom to indulge in travel and hobbies. Retirees worldwide are redefining retirement, creating a fulfilling phase of life where you can pursue passions, contribute to society, and enjoy personal fulfillment and financial stability.

You have the freedom to explore income-generating opportunities aligned with your interests. Consider teaching, coaching, writing, or offering specialized services in areas that fire up your passions. This provides a source of income and allows you to continue engaging in activities you love, bringing fulfillment and purpose to your retirement years. When deciding whether to pursue a profitable hobby, consider the following to make the decision easier:

- Make a list of hobbies and interests that you enjoy the most, and where your skills lie. Think about things you have the most experience or expertise in. Remember, combining our ability to create products and to teach others new skills can have a great earning capability.

- Browse the web to check the demand and profitability of potential hobbies. Check how popular certain jobs or hobbies are, and how much you can earn doing them. This will help you decide whether or not a job is a worthwhile investment.

- List the resources you need to pursue your desired hobby. Write down the initial investments, as well as ongoing costs, equipment, supplies, and whether or not you will need training or certifications. Check all that against your budget, and of course, potential returns.

- Before fully committing to your hobby, consider dipping your toes in and testing the water. Make a couple of products and see if there will be interested buyers, what their thoughts are, and whether or not you find the work worth the cost. Sometimes a hobby is so much fun that returning even a fraction of the investment is satisfying enough. In that case, you should consider whether or not you can sustain your hobby in the long run.

- Get the right training. If you are mastering a new hobby or skill, then you may need a bit of practice, training, or a class.

- Reflect on how the chosen hobby aligns with your desired retirement goals and lifestyle.

Think about whether or not it allows enough flexibility, or if it requires too much time. Think about how it will affect your work-life balance so that you are still able to enjoy your retirement while generating income.

● Once you decide to try to earn income from your hobby, make a plan for growth and adaptation. Stay open to learning, evolving, and exploring new opportunities.

Ultimately, be sure the part-time hobby or interest you choose brings you satisfaction, whether you make profit from it or not. This is important to remember because no amount of market research can tell you for sure whether your investment will pay off. If you invest time and resources into a hobby that doesn't bring you much joy, then not even profits will make up for the lost leisure.

Remote Work, Gig Economy, and Online Earning

Embrace the exciting possibilities that technology brings! You, as retirees, have incredible opportunities to earn from the cozy comfort of your own homes. Imagine the freedom of remote work, where you can work from anywhere, at your own pace. Learn more about the gig economy, where you can choose projects that align with your schedule and passions.

Now, you might be hearing "gig economy" for the first time. While remote work means working from home or some other place outside the office, the gig economy is a slang term that describes more independent, freelance work on temporary or short-term jobs, or "gigs." Gigs are becoming increasingly popular because there is both high supply and high demand for these jobs. More people want to catch opportunities to earn spare cash, while employers and individuals delegate a lot more work than they used to.

The world is your oyster, and the possibilities are endless. You can consider catering, babysitting, dog walking, gardening, cooking for other people, driving, and much more. Aside from that, don't forget about the extra income streams from paid survey websites and other online earning platforms.

To decide whether remote temporary jobs are for you, consider their main attributes, benefits, and shortcomings:

- Flexibility. Most remote gigs are easily done at home from your computer, kitchen, or vehicle. Some can even be done while you're on vacation. You choose the time and amount of work hours in a day.

- Adjustability. You can try catering, food delivery, babysitting, online jobs, and so much more. The best thing about gigs is that you can move from one to the next without much hassle.

- Caution. Yes, it is important to be cautious and think about risks associated with some parts of the gig economy. You might be spending less time outside than you should, especially if you're working from home. If you're working outside, you will meet plenty of strangers, which can be a benefit or a risk.

- Company. Gigs allow you to spend more time with folks of various ages and interests, at the pace that works best for you.

- Profits. Earnings from remote and part-time gigs can be significant, but often aren't reliable. If you're choosing to work because you need to meet a certain monthly quota, gigs might not be the best option.

Continuing Education and Training

Investing in ongoing education and training can be a fantastic way for you to enhance your skills or acquire new ones, opening up exciting income-earning opportunities. These are also great places to lend your knowledge as a mentor or a coach. You could take courses, attend workshops, or pursue certifications in areas that interest you. By staying updated and relevant, you'll position yourself for new career paths or even entrepreneurial ventures. Keep growing and thriving!

You have a variety of education and training options to choose from. Here are the most retirement-friendly sources:

Colleges and Universities

Check out universities and colleges that offer special programs for retirees. See if they offer continuing education courses or senior learning initiatives. Programs like these allow you to pursue your interests and learn new skills in a relaxed and supportive environment.

The Internet

The internet provides a wealth of education, including online courses. Check out hubs like Coursera, Udemy, and Khan Academy. They offer an abundance of courses on various topics, and many of them are also free of charge.

Community Centers

Local community centers often offer classes and workshops tailored to the needs and interests of retirees. These centers provide opportunities to learn new skills, engage in hobbies, and socialize with like-minded individuals.

Volunteering

Engaging in volunteer work can be a valuable learning experience. It allows you to contribute to your community while gaining new skills and knowledge. Many organizations offer training programs for volunteers, ensuring that you have the necessary skills to make a meaningful impact.

Professional Associations

You can join professional associations or clubs revolving around your major interests and hobbies. These organizations sometimes provide educational resources, learning opportunities, and training programs specifically designed for retirees.

Your best education and training options depend on your interests, preferences, and the amount of time and effort that you wish to dedicate. Before making your decision, explore different options and choose those that best align with your passions and desired learning outcomes.

Social and Emotional Benefits

Continuing to earn during retirement offers more than just financial benefits. It also provides social connections, a sense of purpose, and mental stimulation, all of which enhance overall well-being and life satisfaction. By staying engaged in work or income-generating activities, you maintain social connections with colleagues, clients, or customers, fostering a sense of belonging and community. Additionally, having a sense of purpose and contributing to society through work provides a fulfilling and meaningful experience. Moreover, the mental stimulation that comes from learning new skills, solving problems, and staying intellectually active helps keep your mind sharp and promotes cognitive well-being.

You have the opportunity to broaden your networks and forge new connections by getting involved in work-related activities or exploring entrepreneurial ventures. This can lead to exciting opportunities for collaboration, mentorship, and personal development. Furthermore, continuing to earn has a positive impact on those around you. As a financially secure and emotionally fulfilled retiree, you have the power to support your loved ones, make a difference in your community, and participate in meaningful philanthropic activities. Prioritizing your own well-being can create a positive impact on the lives of those who are dear to you.

The ever-evolving world of retirement presents a multitude of exciting opportunities to earn on your own terms. Embrace the financial perks, transition slowly from full-time work, and take the chance to pursue your passions and interests. Consider the possibility of remote work and the gig economy, and keep learning and growing through continued education and training. These options not only boost your financial security but also keep you socially connected and provide a deep sense of purpose and well-being throughout your retirement journey. So go ahead, explore these amazing possibilities, and make your retirement years truly fulfilling!

However, remember that continuing to work in retirement is a decision that shouldn't be made lightly. You have earned your rest and comforts, and it's important to consider whether the work will benefit your health and well-being in the long term. If working may lead to potentially higher medical bills in the future, it might be wise to slow down.

Carefully consider what you want, need, and like. The less you need, the more emphasis should be on what you want and what works for you. Sometimes, your needs might be better met not by earning more, but by monetizing your existing assets and finding ways to spend less. In the next chapter, you will learn more about evaluating your housing needs and leveraging your assets to your advantage.

Chapter 4:

Housing and Lifestyle

Retirement is a wonderful opportunity for you to reevaluate your housing needs and preferences. You can think about downsizing, relocating, or even exploring alternative housing options such as retirement communities or age-restricted neighborhoods. Consider factors like accessibility, maintenance, amenities, and cost when making your decision. By exploring different housing choices, you may discover ways to enhance your retirement experience.

Although they may appear cumbersome, analyzing your housing needs and lifestyle choices are necessary steps in early retirement planning. You don't need to take immediate action, but having thoughtful and uplifting discussions about your housing options is essential. Due to fluctuations in the real estate market, changes in the financial landscape as years go by, and changes in personal housing needs and preferences, many retirees who didn't move from their homes wish they had. Don't make the same mistake. Consider the most important aspects of housing in more detail before retiring. This chapter will help you review key housing aspects and help you make an informed decision.

Assessing and Evaluating Housing Needs

When considering your housing needs, focus on what brings you happiness and fulfillment. Factors to consider include your preferred climate, proximity to family, access to recreational activities, immersion in cultural amenities, and the opportunity to build strong social networks. Prioritizing social connections and community involvement can greatly enhance your overall well-being. Additionally, take financial factors into account. Evaluate the costs associated with home ownership such as insurance, taxes, and maintenance. Ensure that your housing expenses align with your retirement plan, striking a balance between financial goals and enjoyment.

Another important aspect is health care access. Consider the proximity and availability of health care facilities and services, as well as the potential need for long-term medical care and support in the future. Prioritizing easy access to health care resources provides peace of mind for you and your loved ones.

By considering health care and housing factors, you can make well-informed decisions when evaluating your needs. Here are some important considerations for you to think about:

Community Amenities and Services

Research the amenities and services offered by various housing options. Consider proximity to grocery stores, health care facilities, fun activities, and cultural attractions that match your interests and lifestyle. Also, consider the parking spaces for ease of mobility. Think about what kind of a neighborhood you'd like to live in, paying special attention to noise from clubs or nightlife, traffic density, and other relevant aspects.

Social Connections and Community Involvement

Assess the possibilities for social connections and community involvement in various housing options. Explore communities or neighborhoods that offer social activities, clubs, or events tailored to your interests. These provide opportunities to connect with like-minded individuals and create meaningful bonds.

Financial Planning for Housing

Include housing expenses in your overall retirement financial plan. Consider property taxes, homeowner's insurance, maintenance costs, and how housing expenses might change over time. Ensure that your housing choices match your budget and long-term financial goals.

Emotional Considerations

Reflect on the emotional aspects of your housing choices. Consider how different housing options can impact your sense of belonging, independence, and overall well-being. Envision the kind of environment that will bring you joy and fulfillment in your retirement years.

Seek Professional Advice

Consulting with a financial advisor or retirement specialist is a fantastic idea! They can offer valuable guidance on housing options and their financial implications. They'll help you evaluate the costs and benefits of different choices, ensuring that your housing decisions align with your overall retirement plan. You're in good hands!

Personal Preferences and Priorities

Consider your personal preferences and priorities as you make housing decisions. Reflect on what truly matters to you in terms of location, lifestyle, and the kind of community or environment you envision for your retirement years.

Housing and Lifestyle Options

Making a decision regarding where you'll live isn't easy as retirement approaches, but it is necessary. Many retirees don't want to change the lifestyle they're used to, and by the time they realize that their needs have changed, uprooting becomes a lot more difficult. Because of this, you should muster the courage to look into the housing possibilities that may help shape an easier, happier life in retirement. When thinking about housing and lifestyle options, you have a few exciting choices to explore.

Stay Home

One of your options is aging in place, where you get to stay in your beloved home and embark on thrilling home projects, improvements, and modifications. By creating a space that's not just comfortable but also safe, you can age gracefully and maintain your independence.

If you're pondering staying in place, think about these key aspects:

- Assess your home and identify any necessary modifications to make it more age-friendly. You can install grab bars in bathrooms, improve lighting, or create a step-free entrance. Adapting your home to meet your changing needs will enhance safety and ease mobility.

- Evaluate the accessibility of your home and its surroundings. Consider factors such as stairs, narrow doorways or uneven surfaces that may pose challenges as you age. Ensuring that your home is easily navigable promotes independence and reduces the risk of accidents.

- Think about the availability of social support networks in your community. Consider proximity to family, friends, and neighbors who can provide assistance or companionship when you need it. Maintaining social connections is crucial for emotional well-being and a sense of belonging.

- Assess the availability and proximity of health care services in your area. Consider the accessibility of doctors, specialists, hospitals, and other medical facilities. Having convenient access to health care resources is essential for managing your health effectively.

- Evaluate the transportation options in your area, in case you may need them. Consider whether public transportation, ride-sharing services, or accessible transportation are readily available. Access to reliable transportation helps you maintain an active and independent lifestyle.

- Consider your home's ongoing maintenance requirements. Can you manage the upkeep, or will you need assistance? Planning for regular maintenance and repairs helps ensure that your home remains in good condition.

- Explore the amenities and services available in your community. Look for recreational facilities, cultural activities, shopping centers, parks, and other things that align with your interests and preferences. Access to these amenities enhances your quality of life and provides opportunities for engagement.

By considering these important aspects, you can make an informed decision about staying in place for your retirement years. Create a safe, comfortable, and supportive environment that allows you to age gracefully and enjoy a fulfilling lifestyle.

Downsize or Rightsize

Another option to consider is downsizing and rightsizing. Imagine the wonderful advantages of reducing the size of your home. Picture yourself enjoying the benefits of reduced maintenance effort and costs, unlocking equity, and embracing a simpler lifestyle. Find out if a smaller, more manageable home would be the perfect fit for your retirement dreams. It can open up new possibilities and enhance your overall quality of life.

When you're thinking about downsizing and rightsizing, here are a few key points to consider:

Lifestyle and Needs

Assess your current lifestyle and future needs. Consider the space requirements that will best suit your retirement lifestyle. Think about whether a smaller, more manageable home aligns with your preferences and goals. Evaluate your priorities and determine what features and amenities are essential for your well-being and enjoyment.

Financial Implications

Consider the potential cost savings associated with a smaller home, such as reduced mortgage payments, property taxes, and utility bills. Additionally, downsizing can potentially unlock equity that can be used to support your retirement plans or other financial goals.

Maintenance Effort and Costs

Assess the maintenance work and costs associated with your current home. Downsizing can often mean reducing the time and resources required for home maintenance and repairs. Would a smaller home alleviate some of the burdens of upkeep, allowing you to enjoy a simpler and more carefree lifestyle?

Emotional Attachment

How emotionally attached are you to your current home? Downsizing may involve letting go of sentimental attachments and embracing a new living environment. Consider how you would feel about leaving your current home and whether you are ready for the emotional transition that comes with downsizing.

Location and Community

Think about where your new home potentially could be. Consider factors such as proximity to family and friends, access to amenities, and the overall atmosphere of the neighborhood. Ensure that the new location aligns with your desired lifestyle and provides the social connections and support you seek.

Accessibility

Consider accessibility features that will allow you to age in place comfortably. Look for homes with features like single-level living, wider doorways, and accessible bathrooms. Prioritizing accessibility can help ensure that your new home remains suitable for your needs as you age.

Long-Term Plans and Goals

Consider your long-term plans and goals. Think about how downsizing fits into your retirement plan and whether it fits your vision for the future. Evaluate whether a smaller home will accommodate any potential changes in your health, mobility, or lifestyle as you age.

Relocation

In Chapter 2, we reviewed the financial aspects of relocation. However, moving to another home, and potentially changing neighborhoods and towns, doesn't only have potential financial benefits. You also may be able to move to a quieter, safer area with infrastructure and amenities that are better suited to your needs.

By considering these housing situations, you can make an informed decision about downsizing and rightsizing that suits your needs, preferences, and financial situation. Find a new home—or stay in the one you're in. Just make sure it supports your desired lifestyle and allows you to enjoy your retirement to the fullest.

Alternative Accommodations and Living Arrangements

If you decide to move, you have plenty of options to consider. The ultimate decision remains entirely yours. Here are a couple of accommodation arrangements to think about:

Retirement Communities

Explore the wonderful world of retirement communities, villages, and homes! So many options are waiting for you to discover them. Imagine vibrant, active adult communities, cozy age-restricted communities, and supportive assisted living facilities. You can also find the perfect fit in continuing care retirement communities and peaceful rest homes. These communities offer services and social opportunities. It may be time to embark on a new chapter of your life in a retirement community.

Multigenerational Living

Consider the wonderful option of living with your beloved family members like your adult children or grandchildren. You can choose to live independently on the same property or share the same home, creating lasting memories together. Embrace the countless benefits of intergenerational relationships and the support they bring into your life.

Co-Housing

Explore the concept of co-housing, where you get to live together in a supportive community setting. Imagine sharing resources and expenses and forming meaningful social connections. Co-housing is all about you and other retirees coming together to create a multigenerational community that fosters a strong sense of togetherness and support.

Home Sharing

Consider exploring the possibilities of home sharing, where you can welcome like-minded individuals as roommates or boarders. This not only brings companionship but also offers an opportunity to earn some extra income. Another interesting option is to open your doors to international students, allowing for cultural exchange and making the most of your valuable life experience.

Renting vs. Owning

Consider the advantages and disadvantages of renting versus owning a home. Think about things like financial flexibility, long-term security, maintenance responsibilities, and lifestyle preferences. Assess which option suits your retirement goals and circumstances the best.

Home Equity and Reverse Mortgages

You can explore how to use home equity in retirement! Discover the potential of reverse mortgages and other financial tools that can help you make the most of your golden years. Take a closer look at the risks and benefits associated with these options and remember to seek professional advice when considering them. Embrace the possibilities and embark on a journey toward a secure and fulfilling retirement!

Travel and Seasonal Living

Explore the enchantment of long-term travel or seasonal living. Discover the excitement of options like living in an RV or motor home, owning a second home in your dream location, engaging in house exchanges, volunteering abroad, or embarking on exciting seasonal contract work experiences. Uncover how these incredible opportunities align with your unique lifestyle and retirement aspirations.

Long-Term Care Considerations

Thinking about the possibility of needing long-term care during your retirement? Let's explore these options together and find the best fit for you! Here are some key steps:

Research and Visit Facilities

Take the time to research and visit various long-term care facilities such as nursing homes and assisted living communities. Consider factors like location, services provided, staff qualifications, safety measures, and the overall atmosphere.

Assess Your Needs

Evaluate your current and potential future needs for long-term care. Take into account factors such as medical conditions, mobility, assistance required for daily activities, and social interaction opportunities. This will help determine the level of care you may need and the type of facility that suits you best.

Plan for the Future

Ensure your financial well-being by exploring options like long-term care insurance, government assistance programs, and personal savings. Consult with a financial advisor to understand your choices and create a plan that fits your financial situation.

Understand What Services Are Offered

Have a clear understanding of the services provided by different long-term care facilities. These can include assistance with daily activities, medication management, meal preparation, social activities, and medical support.

Staff-to-Resident Ratio

Ask about the staff-to-resident ratio at the facilities you're considering. A lower ratio often means more personalized care and attention for residents.

What Do Current Residents Say?

Talk with current residents and their families to learn about their experiences and the quality of care provided. Ask about any concerns they may have to gain a firsthand, more clear perspective.

Review Contracts and Policies

Carefully review the contracts, policies, and procedures of the long-term care facility. Pay attention to details such as admission criteria, fees, discharge policies, and resident rights. Seek clarification if needed.

Consider Proximity to Loved Ones

Take into account the location, and the proximity of the facility to your loved ones. Being near family and friends can provide emotional support and make visits easier.

Social Engagement

Choose facilities that offer a variety of social activities, outings, and opportunities to connect with fellow residents. Nurturing social connections is important for your mental and emotional well-being.

Involve Loved Ones

Include your loved ones in discussions and decisions regarding long-term care. Their input and support can provide valuable insights and make the process more meaningful.

Take Your Time

Choosing a long-term care facility is a significant decision. Ask questions, gather information, and make an informed choice that meets your needs and preferences.

Remember to think about your housing needs and preferences with a smile on your face! Consider your financial situation, your dreams for the future, and your long-term plans. Don't hesitate to reach out to professionals for advice when you need it. And don't forget to explore all the wonderful housing and lifestyle options out there to find the perfect fit for your retirement adventure! Remember, when it comes to housing and lifestyle choices, it's all about you! Take the time to explore and evaluate your options, seeking advice when necessary. By making informed decisions, you'll be able to enhance your retirement experience and create a life that truly suits you.

Chapter 5:

Health and Wellness

Prioritizing your health and wellness during retirement is crucial to continuing to enjoy an active, balanced, and fulfilling lifestyle. In this chapter, we'll dive into different aspects of health and wellness that are vital for you incredible retirees. Let's jump right in and explore these essential points together!

Healthy Aging

Approach the journey of aging with a positive mindset, resilience, and adaptability. Embrace the beautiful changes that come with age and prioritize your overall well-being in every aspect of your life. You've got this! Healthy aging for retirees involves adopting lifestyle changes that promote your physical, mental, and emotional well-being as you age.

Regular physical exercise has so many amazing perks for you! It boosts your cardiovascular health, enhances your strength and flexibility, improves your balance to keep you steady and safe, and lowers your chances of developing chronic diseases. Keep moving and enjoy the incredible benefits!

Low-impact activities are perfect for you! Embrace the fun of swimming, water walking or water aerobics, biking, tai chi, yoga, and walking. They're all great options to keep you active and feeling fantastic! Discover the fun of sports and competitive activities! You can try games like pickleball, bowling, golf, and tennis. You could even join the Masters and Veterans games for some friendly competition. Plus, some exercise and balance classes are tailored just for you.

Maintaining physical health during retirement is a breeze when you follow these useful guidelines (National Institute of Diabetes and Digestive and Kidney Diseases, 2019):

- Prioritize balance and flexibility. Exercises that enhance balance and flexibility will not only reduce the risk of falls, but also will help you maintain your mobility. Activities like yoga, tai chi, or Pilates are known to improve your balance, posture, and flexibility.

- Maintain a healthy weight. Enjoy a balanced diet and stay active with regular physical activity. Remember, you can always seek personalized guidance on nutrition and weight management from a health care professional or registered dietitian.

- Prioritize your safety while exercising! Remember to warm up before each session, use proper form and technique, and listen to your body. If you have any health concerns or conditions, consult a health care professional before starting a new exercise program. Stay safe and enjoy your workouts!

- Stay hydrated! Make sure you drink enough water throughout the day to keep yourself hydrated. Remember, dehydration can have a negative impact on your overall health and well-being, so make drinking water a regular habit.

- Get regular checkups to keep your health in check and address any concerns you may have. Make sure to stay up to date with vaccinations, screenings, and preventive care. Remember, keeping yourself healthy allows you to make retirement everything it can be!

- Take good care of your joints. Make sure to protect your joints by practicing proper body mechanics and using assistive devices if needed. Remember, you're in control! Avoid putting excessive strain on your joints and always listen to your body's signals to prevent overexertion.

- Practice good posture. Maintaining good posture supports your spinal health and prevents musculoskeletal issues. Remember to be mindful of your posture while you're sitting, standing, and walking. Also incorporate exercises that strengthen your core muscles to help support proper posture.

- Get enough sleep. Prioritize quality rest to support your overall health and well-being. Aim to get seven to eight hours of sleep per night and establish a consistent sleep routine. Ensure your sleep environment is comfortable and practice good sleep hygiene.

- Listen to your body and pay close attention to its signals. Adjust your activities accordingly, making sure to rest when needed, and don't push yourself beyond your limits. If you ever experience any pain or discomfort during exercise, consult a health care professional.

Your Diet Makes the Difference

In your retirement journey, make the time for the wonderful world of wholesome foods, portion control, and mindful eating. Discover the significance of nourishing your body and mind with a well-balanced diet. And guess what? Some exciting recent research backs this up (King & Xiang, 2017; National Institute of Diabetes and Digestive and Kidney Diseases, 2019). So, are you ready to embark on this delicious adventure? Let's go!

Eat a Balanced Diet

You can enjoy a delightful array of nutrient-packed foods to nourish your body. Include a colorful assortment of fruits and vegetables, lots of whole grains, lean proteins, and nourishing fats in your diet. Embrace a well-balanced eating plan that offers vital vitamins, minerals, and fiber to keep you feeling vibrant and healthy.

Portion Control

Pay attention to portion sizes to avoid overeating. Your metabolism may slow down with age, so adjust portion sizes to maintain a healthy weight.

Stay Hydrated

Stay hydrated and keep your spirits high by drinking plenty of water throughout the day! Remember, as you age, it's important to stay on top of your hydration game. Aim for at least 8 cups of water daily, unless your health care professional suggests otherwise. Cheers to a well-hydrated you!

Focus on Fiber

Include fiber-rich foods like whole grains, fruits, vegetables, and legumes in your diet. They can help support your digestive health and prevent constipation, which can be more common as we age.

Eat Enough Protein

Ensure you get enough protein to keep your muscles healthy and prevent muscle loss that can happen as you age. Make sure to include lean meats, poultry, fish, eggs, dairy products, legumes, and plant-based protein sources in your diet.

Choose Healthy Fats

Opt for sources of healthy fats like avocados, nuts, seeds, and olive oil. Remember to limit saturated and trans fats, which can be found in fried foods, processed snacks, and fatty meats. Make choices that support your well-being and keep you feeling great!

Limit Sodium Intake

Reduce your sodium intake to support your heart health and manage your blood pressure. Say no to processed foods, canned soups, and salty snacks. Instead, spice up your meals with herbs, spices, and other delicious flavorings!

Consider Calcium and Vitamin D

You may benefit from boosting your calcium and vitamin D intake to maintain strong and healthy bones. Consider incorporating dairy products, fortified plant-based milk, leafy greens, and fatty fish into your diet. Consult a health care professional for personalized recommendations.

Mindful Eating

Practice mindful eating by paying attention to your hunger and fullness cues. Take your time while eating, savor the delicious flavors, and delight in your meals in a peaceful and serene setting.

Seek Professional Guidance

Consulting with a registered dietitian or health care professional who specializes in nutrition for older adults is a great idea. They can offer you personalized advice tailored to your specific needs and health conditions, and account for any medication interactions.

Remember, individual dietary needs vary, so consider your personal health conditions, medications, and any specific dietary restrictions. A health care professional can provide you with tailored guidance to help you maintain a healthy diet that suits your unique circumstances.

Mental, Cognitive, and Emotional Well-Being

As relaxing as retirement can be, the lack of engagement and stimulation that comes from work and daily socializing can, over time, take a toll on your cognitive, emotional, and mental well-being. While your overall health depends on the combination of genes, habits, lifestyle, and much more, there's still a lot you can do to keep your mind sharp and your mindset hopeful and optimistic. Doing so will help you process changes and adapt better, feel good, and be more focused and energized. In this section, you'll learn how to care for your emotional, mental, and cognitive well-being by keeping your mind sharp, practicing mindfulness, and reaching out to support systems.

Maintaining Brain Health

Engage in mentally stimulating activities to keep your brain sharp. Challenge yourself with things like reading books, solving puzzles, playing strategy games, learning a new language, or playing a musical instrument. These activities stimulate different areas of your brain and promote mental agility.

Learn new skills to keep your brain engaged and adaptable. Take classes or workshops in subjects that interest you, such as painting, cooking, photography, or computer skills. Learning new things not only stimulates your brain but also gives you a sense of accomplishment and personal growth.

Embrace mind-challenging adventures to step out of your comfort zone. Travel to new places, engage in cultural activities, or participate in intellectually stimulating events like lectures or seminars. Exploring unfamiliar environments and ideas keeps your brain active and curious (Brumberg, 2023).

Managing Stress

Incorporate relaxation techniques into your daily routine to manage stress effectively. Try deep breathing exercises, progressive muscle relaxation, guided imagery, or meditation. Find a technique you like and practice it regularly to promote relaxation and reduce stress levels.

Cultivate mindfulness by being fully present in the moment and being aware of your thoughts and feelings without judging them. Embrace mindful breathing or mindful walking to help manage stress and promote a sense of calm and grounding. Make mindfulness a part of your daily life to reduce stress and enhance overall well-being.

Engage in activities that are fun and relaxing. Indulge in hobbies, spend time in nature, listen to music, practice yoga or tai chi, take warm baths, or enjoy a good book. Prioritize self-care and make time for activities that help you unwind and recharge (Brumberg, 2023).

Seeking Support

Remember, you're never alone on this journey. Whenever you need it, reach out for support. You can find solace through counseling or therapy, or by joining nurturing communities that uplift your mental and emotional well-being (Brumberg, 2023).

- Counseling or therapy. If you're ever feeling overwhelmed or facing emotional challenges, remember that seeking professional help can make a world of difference. You deserve support and guidance to navigate difficult times and improve your mental and emotional well-being. Consider reaching out to a trained therapist who can provide you with the strategies and support you need.

- Supportive communities: Connect with supportive communities that share your interests or experiences. Join clubs, groups, or organizations that foster a sense of belonging and provide opportunities for social interaction. Engaging with like-minded individuals will offer you support, understanding, and a strong sense of community.

- Reach out to loved ones. You should never hesitate to reach out to your family members, friends, or other people you trust whenever you need support. Sharing your thoughts and feelings with your loved ones can bring you comfort, an empathetic ear, and a fresh perspective.

Benefits of Social Connections

Embrace the power of social connections and discover how they can brighten your life! Explore the incredible benefits of nurturing existing relationships and forging new ones. Additionally, look into exciting hobbies, interests, and social groups that bring fun and fulfillment to your journey of health and well-being. You are the architect of your own vibrant social network, and there are many benefits to remaining socially active in retirement (Burholt et al., 2020).

Enhanced Emotional Well-Being

Social connections are key to promoting emotional well-being. By nurturing existing relationships and building new ones, you can experience a sense of belonging, support, and companionship. Engaging in meaningful social interactions combats loneliness, reduces stress, and improves your overall mood and happiness.

Increased Cognitive Stimulation

Your social connections provide valuable cognitive stimulation, keeping your mind sharp. Engaging in conversations, discussions, and activities with others challenges your brain, promotes mental agility, and even helps prevent cognitive decline. Socializing exposes you to new ideas, perspectives, and knowledge, and fosters continuous learning and intellectual growth.

Improved Physical Health

Strange as it may sound, your social connections have a positive impact on your physical health. Engaging in social activities often involves physical movement, encouraging you to stay active. Additionally, the social support from friends and loved ones can motivate you and hold you accountable for maintaining a healthy lifestyle, getting regular exercise, and making nutritious food choices.

Sense of Purpose and Fulfillment

Social connections bring a sense of purpose and fulfillment during retirement. Engaging in hobbies, interests, and social groups that align with your passions and values brings joy, a sense of belonging, and a renewed sense of purpose. It offers opportunities to share experiences, contribute to the community, and make a positive impact in the lives of others.

Opportunities for Learning and Growth

Your social connections provide opportunities for learning and personal growth. Engaging with a diverse group of people exposes you to different perspectives, cultures, and experiences. This broadens your horizons, challenges your assumptions, and fosters personal development.

Support System

Your social connections create a reliable support system during challenging times. Friends, family, and social groups offer emotional support, practical assistance, and a listening ear. Having a strong support network helps you navigate life transitions, cope with stress, and find comfort and encouragement.

Tips for Building and Nurturing Social Connections

- Join clubs, organizations, or community groups that align with your interests and hobbies. It's a fantastic way to meet people who share your passions and have a great time together.

- Volunteer for causes that mean a lot to you. Not only will you make a difference, but you'll also meet incredible people who care about the same things.

- Attend social events, workshops, or classes where you can connect with others who have similar interests. Take a chance, have fun and forge new friendships.

- Stay connected with your loved ones through regular phone calls, video chats, or in-person visits. They're wonderful ways to nurture your relationships and create lasting memories.

- Explore online communities and social media platforms that cater to your interests. You'll find a vibrant community of like-minded people to connect with and share your passions.

- Consider joining support groups or organizations specifically created for retirees.

You'll meet people who understand your life stage and can offer support and companionship.

- Embrace the opportunity to make new friends and take the lead in social interactions. Reach out, make plans, and invite others to join you in activities or outings. You never know what amazing connections you'll make!

Remember, building and nurturing social connections takes time and effort. You should be patient, open-minded, and proactive in seeking opportunities to connect with others. Feel the power of social connections and create your own vibrant social network that will bring joy, fulfillment, and a sense of belonging to your retirement journey.

Preventative Health Care

Regular checkups, vaccinations, and screenings are key to staying on top of your health game. They help detect potential health issues early on, giving you a better chance of maintaining your well-being. Embrace healthy habits like steering clear of smoking, and enjoying alcohol in moderation. These choices can greatly influence your long-term health and happiness.

These tips can help you make the most of regular checkups, appointments, and medication management:

- Create a health care schedule. Make a calendar to keep track of your upcoming appointments, including checkups and specialist visits. Remember to note the date, time, and location of each appointment.

- Set reminders. Use your phone, computer, or a physical calendar to set reminders for your appointments. Set multiple reminders in advance to make sure you don't forget.

- Enlist a support system. Ask a family member, friend, or caregiver to help you manage your appointments. They can assist with scheduling and transportation, and accompany you to visits.

- Use technology. Take advantage of smartphone apps or online tools that can send you appointment reminders and help you keep track of your medications.

- Keep a medications list: Maintain an updated list of all your medications, including the name, dosage, and frequency. This will help you remember what medications you need to take and when.

- Use pill organizers. Get pill organizers with compartments for each day of the week. Fill them in advance to ensure you take the right medications at the right times. Consider using alarms or reminders to help you remember.

- Simplify medication management. Talk to your health care provider about simplifying your medication regimen if it's challenging to keep up with multiple medications. They may be able to adjust dosages or consolidate medications to make it easier for you.

- Ask for help with transportation. If transportation is a challenge, explore options like public transportation, community services, or rides with family or friends. Some health care facilities may also offer transportation services for seniors.

- Communicate with your health care provider. If you're having trouble keeping up with appointments or managing your medications, don't hesitate to talk to your health care provider. They can provide guidance and solutions, or make adjustments to meet your needs.

- Consider tele-health options. Look into tele-health or virtual health care options, especially for routine checkups or follow-up appointments. These can be convenient alternatives that eliminate the need for transportation and allow you to consult with your health care provider from home.

Remember, open communication with your health care provider is important to ensure you receive the care and support you need.

Wellness and Mind-Body Practices

Incorporate mind-body practices like yoga, meditation, tai chi, or mindfulness into your retirement routine. These practices can bring you relaxation, reduce stress, and enhance your overall well-being. Alternative practices such as massage, acupuncture, homeopathy, or Oriental medicine can complement traditional approaches to wellness.

Here's a guide to mind-body practices like wellness, mindfulness, and meditation. Let's explore some tips and considerations together!

- Start with small steps. Begin by incorporating small, achievable practices into your daily routine. You can take a few minutes each day to focus on your breath or engage in a short mindfulness exercise.

- Explore different practices. Experiment with various mind-body practices to find what resonates with you. You can try mindfulness meditation, yoga, tai chi, qigong, or other relaxation techniques. Discover what brings you a sense of calm and peace.

- Create a dedicated space for yourself. Designate a cozy and peaceful corner in your home where you can indulge in mind-body exercises. This special spot will be your personal sanctuary, a haven for relaxation and deep contemplation.

- Set aside regular practice time. Schedule dedicated time for mind-body practices each day. Be consistent, even if you can only spare a few minutes. As you become more comfortable, gradually increase the duration. Remember, every small step counts!

- Seek guidance. Consider attending classes or workshops, or find experienced instructors or practitioners. They can offer you valuable insights, techniques, and support to enhance your mind-body practice.

- Practice deep breathing. Deep breathing exercises can help you calm your mind and relax your body. Take slow, deep breaths, and focus on the sensation of the breath entering and leaving your body.

- Cultivate mindfulness in your daily activities. Embrace the present moment and bring mindfulness into your everyday life. Fully engage in activities like eating, walking, or even washing dishes. Be fully present and savor the experience, embracing the sensations that surround you.

- Practice self-compassion. Be kind and gentle with yourself as you explore mind-body practices. Let go of judgment and expectations. Embrace self-compassion and accept that your practice will evolve over time.

- Practice guided meditations using apps, recordings, or online resources that can assist you in your meditation practice. They can provide structure and guidance, especially if you're new to meditation.

- Stay consistent and patient, my friend! Mind-body practices are all about finding your rhythm and sticking with it. Remember, results may not come right away, but if you keep at it, you'll start to see the benefits unfold. So be patient with yourself, embrace the journey, and enjoy every step of the way!

- Keep in mind that you can personalize mind-body practices to suit your preferences and needs. Explore various techniques, stay open to the process, and discover what brings you the most fun and fulfillment.

In this chapter, you learned how to maintain your health for a vibrant lifestyle and greater longevity. Taking care of your health and wellness allows you to enjoy a happy retirement, live longer, spend quality time with loved ones, and avoid preventable medical expenses. In the next chapter, you'll learn about how staying involved socially and in your community can improve your retirement experience.

Chapter 6:

Social and Community

Engagement

Staying connected and being part of a community can make the difference between a vibrant retirement and a lonely one. In this chapter, we'll look at how to make friends and get involved in your community. Retirement is not just about enjoying the freedom to pursue your personal interests and passions; it's also about staying connected and being an active part of a community. Now's the time to explore the profound impact that social connections and community involvement can have on our overall well-being and sense of fulfillment during retirement.

As you transition into this new phase of life, don't underestimate the power of human connection. Research consistently shows that maintaining strong social ties is essential for our mental, emotional, and even physical health. In this chapter, you will learn the science behind social connections and discover how nurturing relationships can enhance our happiness, reduce stress, and provide a support system during the ups and downs of retirement. You'll benefit yourself, and bring fun and fulfillment to others through your involvement in the community.

Retirees can contribute time, skills, and wisdom in many ways to make a positive impact on the lives of others. From volunteering for local organizations to participating in community events and initiatives, this chapter will reveal some of the countless opportunities for retirees to leave a lasting legacy and create a sense of purpose that goes beyond personal fulfillment.

Throughout this chapter, you'll get a better idea about how to find deep meaning and connection through your social interactions and community involvement. We'll also provide practical tips and strategies for building and maintaining social connections, overcoming common challenges, and finding the right community activities. We'll also start exploring the transformative power of social connections and community involvement in retirement. Get ready to discover the fun of forging new friendships, making a difference in the lives of others. Creating a connected community enriches your retirement years in ways you never imagined.

Benefits of Social Connections and Involvement

Research consistently demonstrates the significance of staying connected with others throughout your life. These connections greatly benefit your mental health, promote longevity, and foster a sense of belonging. By actively engaging with your community and nurturing relationships, you will discover numerous opportunities for personal growth, meaningful connections, and a sense of purpose.

Maintaining social connections is beneficial for your mental health. By regularly spending time with others, you can reduce feelings of sadness, anxiety, and loneliness. Additionally, engaging in conversations with others provides emotional support, a sense of belonging, and an opportunity to share experiences and challenges. These connections form a support system that helps you cope with stress, enhances your confidence, and improves your overall well-being.

Moreover, research shows that having good friends and strong relationships can help you live longer and lower your chance of getting sick for a long time (Blieszner, Ogletree & Adams, 2019). Additionally, the research states that hanging out with others can make you healthier, boost your immune system, and increase your overall resilience.

Engaging with the community can help you grow as a person. Interacting with different people allows you to see things from their point of view and learn new things. This helps you become more understanding and empathetic. Volunteering or joining group activities in the community can give you a sense of fulfillment and purpose. You can use your skills and talents to make a positive difference, and feel proud of your achievements.

Meaningful relationships are crucial for social connections. Building and nurturing relationships with family, friends, neighbors, and coworkers brings joy, companionship, and a sense of belonging. These relationships provide emotional support, shared experiences, and a feeling of connection. They also offer opportunities for laughter, celebration, and mutual support during tough times. Getting involved in your community and nurturing relationships can help you grow as a person, forge meaningful connections, and find a sense of purpose. By prioritizing social interactions and investing in relationships, you can experience greater happiness, longevity, and fulfillment in life. So, how can you stay engaged and active during retirement? Here are a couple of ideas:

Social Groups

Joining social groups and clubs based on shared interests, hobbies, and activities is a great way to make new friends and feel like you belong. These groups organize clubs for things like gardening, books, singing, dancing, and games. By joining these clubs, you can meet people who have the same hobbies as you. This shared interest is a strong foundation for building meaningful relationships and feeling a sense of camaraderie. There are also international organizations that offer activities and events for people with various interests. These organizations give you the chance to connect with people from different backgrounds and cultures, expand your social network and do things you enjoy.

In these clubs or groups, you can pursue your interests and meet new people. These groups provide a supportive and friendly environment where you can make friends, share ideas, and take part in activities that bring you happiness. Feeling like you belong to a community of people who think like you can greatly improve your overall well-being and quality of life. So, whether it's joining a local gardening club, book club, or choir, or becoming a member of an international organization, exploring these social groups and clubs can open doors to new friendships, shared experiences, and a sense of belonging.

Volunteering, Mentoring, and Coaching

Engaging in meaningful work and supporting others not only helps the community but also brings personal satisfaction. You can share your knowledge, make a positive impact, and find purpose and fulfillment through these activities. We'll touch on volunteering here, and discuss it in more depth In the next chapter.

To begin, you can get involved in local community projects and initiatives. This may involve working with local charities, organizing fundraisers, or participating in neighborhood clean-up and planting efforts. By actively participating in community service, you can contribute to the betterment of your community and feel a sense of pride and connection.

Also consider engaging with local establishments such as libraries, community centers, churches, or colleges. Attend talks, join workshops, or even volunteer if you wish. These places often offer programs and events where you can learn, socialize, and meet like-minded individuals. Other options are to join local government committees, attend community meetings, or advocate for causes you care about. By participating in civic activities, you can have a voice in shaping your community and making a positive impact on issues that are important to you. Furthermore, you can volunteer at schools, become a mentor, or collaborate with youth organizations. These opportunities allow you to share your knowledge and connect with younger generations. Lastly, you can initiate or support neighborhood watch programs, organize social events, and advocate for the needs of your community. These groups foster relationships, neighborly bonds, and a strong sense of attachment.

Cultural and Arts Engagement

Participating in cultural and arts activities is a great way to boost your creativity, appreciate the arts, and meet people with the same interests. By joining arts and book clubs, you can discuss literature, visual arts, music, and more. You can share insights and recommendations, and explore different perspectives.

Watching live theater shows is an amazing experience. Whether it's a play, musical, or dance performance, attending theater allows you to witness the talent and creativity of performers up close. You'll be moved by powerful storytelling, exceptional acting, and mesmerizing stage productions. Additionally, theater venues often provide spaces for socializing before or after the show, so you can connect with other theater lovers.

Exploring museums and galleries allows you to discover a world of art and culture. You can appreciate paintings, sculptures, installations, and other visual art forms. Additionally, museums often offer guided tours, workshops, and special exhibitions that provide deeper insights into the art and the artists. By visiting these cultural spaces, you not only ignite your creativity but also have the opportunity to engage with fellow art enthusiasts. You can even consider joining creative workshops or classes such as painting, pottery, photography, or writing. These workshops provide a supportive environment to explore your creativity, learn new skills, and connect with people who share your passion for the arts.

Cultural festivals and events celebrate diverse artistic expression and traditions. They include music performances, dance shows, art exhibitions, and culinary experiences. By participating in these events, you can immerse yourself in different cultures, appreciate their unique artistic heritage, and connect with people who enjoy exploring the world's diversity.

By actively participating in cultural and arts activities, you can enrich your life in many ways. You can tap into your creativity, find inspiration, and make social connections. You can join arts and book clubs, go to theater shows, visit museums and galleries, take part in creative workshops, or attend cultural festivals. These experiences offer personal growth, help you appreciate art, and connect you with like-minded people. Embrace the vibrant world of arts and culture to enhance your life in countless ways.

Online Communities and Social Media

Online platforms have revolutionized how we connect with others, providing numerous benefits for staying socially engaged. By utilizing online platforms, we can connect with people who share similar interests, offering a multitude of advantages. Whether through forums, social media groups, or specialized websites, these online communities serve as virtual spaces where people can gather to connect, exchange ideas, and engage in discussions. Joining these communities allows you to connect with people who share your passions from all corners of the globe, regardless of your location. They present opportunities to share knowledge, seek advice, and foster meaningful relationships.

Forums and social media groups are perfect for having focused discussions about specific topics or interests. Whether you're part of a group for your favorite hobby, a forum for book lovers, or a social media group dedicated to a specific art form, these platforms allow you to engage in conversations, ask questions, and share experiences. They let you connect with people who share your enthusiasm and can offer valuable insights and recommendations.

Online platforms offer a variety of virtual activities to help you stay socially engaged. You can join virtual book clubs, take online art classes, attend webinars, or go on virtual tours of museums and galleries. Participating allows you to connect with people, learn new skills, and have meaningful experiences from the comfort of your own home. You can stay connected, keep learning, and feel a sense of belonging.

These platforms also provide access to support networks for specific challenges or guidance. Whether it's a group for caregivers, a forum for people with a particular health condition, or an online community for those going through a major life change, these platforms offer a space to connect with others who can provide empathy, understanding, and support. It's an opportunity to share experiences, seek advice, and find comfort in a community that understands your situation.

One great thing about online platforms is that they allow you to connect with people from all over the world. Wherever you are, you can find and engage with people who have similar interests and passions. This global reach expands your social network and exposes you to different perspectives and experiences. Online platforms offer numerous opportunities to connect, share experiences, and stay socially engaged. By joining online communities, participating in forums or social media groups, and taking part in virtual activities, you can feel connected, regardless of your location. Embrace the benefits of online platforms to expand your social network, learn from others, and stay connected in the digital age.

Wellness and Fitness Groups

Joining wellness and fitness groups is a great way to improve your physical health and make new friends. You can join a walking group, try yoga classes, or even give aqua-walking a shot. These groups are all about staying active and connecting with people who have similar health and fitness goals. They provide a supportive environment to help you maintain an active lifestyle. Regular physical activity has many benefits like improving heart health, strength, flexibility, and mood, and reducing the risk of chronic diseases. When you join these groups, you'll stay motivated, receive guidance from instructors or group leaders, and enjoy the accountability that comes from working out with others. Plus, you'll have the chance to meet other active people and form friendships. These groups often organize social activities before or after workouts, so you can chat, share experiences, and support each other on your wellness journeys.

Being part of a wellness or fitness group is like having a supportive squad that keeps you motivated and committed to your health goals. The group members act as cheerleaders, constantly uplifting and inspiring you. They support you during workouts, celebrate your milestones, and provide advice and encouragement. It's like having a fitness family that helps you stay on track. In these groups, you not only receive guidance and instruction from the instructors or leaders, but also learn new techniques and gain wisdom about health and fitness. Additionally, you have the opportunity to learn from other members by exchanging tips, sharing resources, and discovering new ways to take care of yourself.

In this chapter, you learned that social and community engagement not only is enjoyable but also provides an opportunity to socialize while having fun and staying fit. By joining these activities and groups, you can laugh, have a good time, and feel motivated alongside people like yourselves who prioritize a healthy, socially active lifestyle. The benefits of joining social, as well as cultural, wellness and fitness groups are numerous. You can enhance your physical health, forge new friendships, receive support and motivation, acquire new knowledge, and have a fantastic time. Make the most of the groups available in your community and experience the positive impact they can have on your overall well-being. In the next chapter, you will consider ways your family might change when you retire, and consider ideas for strengthening those bonds.

Chapter 7:

Family and Relationships

Many future retirees worry about becoming isolated from their family. Many circumstances could be behind this fear. Younger family members might be starting their careers and forming their own families, so they might move away. You might be coping with the possibility of losing a spouse so you may need to consider a different housing situation. Decades-long friendships might become challenging when one of you becomes ill, less energized, or less mobile.

The idea of retiring might have initially made you think that you'll spend more time with your loved ones, but you might start to worry that you'll be more distant from them now than when you were working. In this chapter, we will try to help ease your fears and remember all the ways you can stay connected to your friends and family.

Prioritizing quality time with family members—including children, grandchildren, and extended family—is crucial for building strong relationships and creating lasting memories.

Quality Time and Family Traditions

Creating family traditions helps foster a sense of belonging and anticipation for future gatherings. Establish traditions like game nights, movie marathons, or annual vacations to bond further and cultivate togetherness. Additionally, engaging in hobbies such as cooking, gardening, or playing sports promotes teamwork and strengthens bonds. Volunteering as a family not only helps others but also teaches important values and strengthens unity.

Plan technology-free time to allow for uninterrupted conversations and quality interactions. Encourage older family members to share stories and anecdotes from the past to help younger generations understand their roots and strengthen the family's collective identity. Celebrating milestones and achievements such as graduations, promotions, or personal accomplishments, shows support and reinforces the importance of family bonds.

Remember to prioritize and make time for these activities to create lasting memories and deepen connections with each other. One suggestion for activities that can help deepen connections is planning regular family outings to parks, museums, or local attractions. You also could set aside specific times for family meals where everyone can gather, share stories, and enjoy each other's company.

Embrace the Supportive Role as Grandparents

Grandparents play a significant role in their grandchildren's lives, providing guidance and support, and creating meaningful connections. They can share wisdom and life experiences, offering valuable insights and guidance. Additionally, grandparents provide unconditional love and support, serving as a source of comfort, encouragement, and reassurance during challenging times. They pass on family traditions, stories, and cultural heritage, preserving family history and strengthening their grandchildren's sense of identity and belonging.

Doing things together—nature walks, picnics, cooking, baking, arts and crafts, storytelling, reading, playing games—promotes bonding and laughter. Grandparents can also teach their grandchildren new skills, fostering intergenerational learning. By embracing their unique role, grandparents create lasting memories and foster meaningful connections that will be cherished for a lifetime.

Caregiving and Support

Retirees often play important roles in providing care and support for aging parents or other family members. They can become primary caregivers, manage daily activities, assist with personal care, coordinate medical appointments, and ensure overall well-being. Retirees also provide valuable emotional support, lending a listening ear, offering comfort, and providing stability and reassurance. They advocate for their loved ones' needs, communicate with health care professionals, manage medications, and navigate the health care system.

Retirees can help with household tasks like cooking, cleaning, and managing finances to alleviate burdens on their aging parents or family members. They also offer companionship, alleviating feelings of loneliness or isolation. Spending quality time together, engaging in conversations, and participating in activities greatly enhance both generations' well-being.

Caregiving, while rewarding, can be time-consuming and impact personal schedules and freedom. It can be emotionally challenging to witness the decline in health or struggles of loved ones. Retirees may experience stress, guilt, or sadness, affecting their own well-being. Personal sacrifices—such as giving up travel plans or hobbies—may be necessary. Adjustments and a shift in priorities are required.

Remember to seek support when needed! Many services are available to help caregivers of people with dementia or terminal illness understand and support their loved ones. They offer much-needed emotional support, and valuable information and assistance tailored to the needs of both the caregiver and their loved ones.

Despite the challenges, caregiving can also bring immense rewards. Retirees have the opportunity to make a positive impact on their loved ones' lives, strengthen family bonds, and experience a sense of fulfillment and purpose. Caregiving provides an opportunity for retirees to learn new skills, gain knowledge about health care and aging, and develop resilience and patience. It can be a transformative experience that enhances personal growth. Retirees in caregiving roles must prioritize self-care, seek support from other family members or support groups, and communicate their needs and limitations. By balancing their own well-being with the care they provide, retirees can navigate the challenges and find fulfillment in their caregiving relationships.

Balancing Independence and Family Support

Maintaining independence in retirement is crucial for well-being and self-identity. Let's explore the significance of independence, strategies for retirees to balance independence with family support, and effective communication and boundary setting within family relationships. Independence empowers retirees to control their lives, make decisions aligned with their values, and pursue their interests. It boosts self-esteem, autonomy, and a positive outlook.

Effective communication is key to balancing independence and family support. Retirees should openly express their needs, concerns, and desires to their family members. This fosters a supportive environment where everyone's perspectives are understood and respected. Assessing capabilities and limitations helps determine when and where support may be needed without compromising independence. Involving family members in decision-making allows you to benefit from their support and input. Collaboration ensures that everyone's voices are heard and respected.

Establishing clear boundaries with family members is essential. This includes defining personal space, privacy, and desired level of involvement. Boundaries foster healthy relationships and prevent conflicts. Retirees can explore community resources and support services to enhance independence. This may include transportation, home maintenance assistance, or tailored social activities. Regular check-ins with family members help maintain a support system without compromising independence. Check-ins can be through phone calls, video chats, or in-person visits, depending on preferences and circumstances. Embracing flexibility and adaptability allows for adjustments and effective problem-solving as needs and circumstances change over time.

Remember, maintaining independence doesn't mean rejecting family support. It means finding a balance that respects autonomy while fostering meaningful connections and collaboration. By practicing open communication, setting boundaries, and using available resources, retirees can successfully navigate this balance and enjoy a fulfilling retirement surrounded by loved ones' support.

Relationships With Adult Children

As you enter the retirement phase, the dynamics of your relationships with your adult children often change. Let's discuss these evolving dynamics and address topics such as boundaries, financial support, inheritance, and maintaining a healthy balance of involvement. Retirees may no longer have the same level of authority or responsibility in the adult-child relationship, so it's important to establish new boundaries that respect each other's autonomy and independence.

During retirement, retirees and adult children may need to navigate discussions about financial support. Retirees should consider their own financial well-being and set realistic expectations for what they can provide. Open and honest communication about financial matters can help manage expectations and avoid misunderstandings. Additionally, retirees may need to address the topic of inheritance and estate planning with their adult children. Have open conversations about wishes, intentions, and any necessary legal arrangements to ensure clarity and minimize potential conflicts in the future.

Maintaining a healthy balance of involvement is key for successful long-term relationships. Retirees may want to offer support and guidance, but they need to respect their adult children's autonomy and allow them to make their own decisions. Likewise, adult children should recognize and appreciate the wisdom and experience that retirees bring.

Respecting individual choices is also essential. As retirees and adult children navigate evolving dynamics, adult children and retirees must respect each other's choices and life paths. This includes respecting different career choices, relationship decisions, and personal values. Acceptance and understanding can help foster a supportive and harmonious relationship. Effective communication is key in maintaining healthy relationships. Both retirees and adult children should practice active listening, empathy, and understanding. This allows for open dialogue, the expression of needs and concerns, and the building of stronger connections.

To strengthen your connection with loved ones, spend plenty of quality time together and create shared experiences. This can include engaging in activities, going on trips, or simply having meaningful conversations. These moments foster connection and help build lasting memories. Support and appreciate each other's efforts and achievements. Celebrating milestones, offering encouragement, and expressing gratitude can strengthen the bond between generations.

Remember, every family dynamic is unique, so approach these evolving relationships with understanding, respect, and open communication. By navigating boundaries, discussing financial matters, and maintaining a healthy balance of involvement, retirees and adult children can cultivate strong and fulfilling relationships that continue to evolve and thrive throughout the retirement phase.

Relationship Enrichment and Emotional Connection

Maintaining and enriching romantic relationships is crucial for retirees to continue experiencing love, connection, and fulfillment. Retirement provides an opportunity for couples to spend more time together, but it also requires adjustment. Spending all your free time together may necessitate adjusting habits and routines for mutual comfort, making retirement a new phase of life. Prioritize quality time by setting aside dedicated moments for activities, date nights, or simply enjoying each other's company. This strengthens the emotional bond and creates opportunities for meaningful conversations.

Collaborate with your family to plan for the future, discussing and setting goals related to travel, personal growth, or retirement aspirations. Planning together strengthens the sense of partnership and shared vision. Maintain open and honest communication with your partner, expressing your feelings, needs, and concerns while actively listening to their perspective. Effective communication builds trust, understanding, and emotional connection.

As physical changes occur with age, retirees may need to adapt and find new ways to maintain intimacy and connection. Explore different forms of physical affection, prioritize self-care, and seek professional advice if needed to address any physical challenges. Nurture emotional and intimate connections by expressing love, appreciation, and affection. Engage in activities that promote emotional intimacy such as sharing memories, writing love letters, or practicing mindfulness together. Encourage and support each other's personal growth and individual interests. Celebrate each other's achievements and provide a safe space for personal exploration and self-expression.

If challenges arise in your relationship, don't hesitate to seek professional help. Couples therapy or counseling can provide guidance, tools, and strategies to navigate difficulties and strengthen your bond. Remember, maintaining and enriching a romantic relationship requires effort, commitment, and ongoing communication. By prioritizing quality time, exploring shared interests, planning together, adapting to physical changes, and nurturing emotional and intimate connections, retirees can continue to experience deep and fulfilling romantic relationships throughout their retirement years.

Documenting Family History

Preserving family history and memories is a meaningful way for retirees to leave a lasting legacy for future generations. It provides a sense of identity, belonging, and connection to one's roots. Additionally, it allows future generations to understand their heritage, learn from the past, and appreciate the experiences and stories of their ancestors. To preserve family memories, start by gathering old photographs, letters, and documents. Record family stories and anecdotes, capturing the memories and experiences of older family members. Organize these materials systematically to ensure easy accessibility and protection.

Digitizing and archiving physical photographs and documents is another option for long-term preservation. This can be done using a scanner or smartphone app designed for digitizing photos. Store the digital files in multiple locations such as external hard drives or cloud storage to safeguard against loss. Creating a family tree is also a great way to visually represent the connections between family members across generations. Online platforms or genealogy software can assist in this process. Include important dates, locations, and relationships to provide a comprehensive overview of your family history.

Online platforms like Ancestry.com, My Heritage, or Legacy can be valuable resources for beginning or updating a family history. They offer tools for building family trees, accessing historical records, and connecting with other researchers who may have shared ancestry. Interviewing older family members is another valuable step. Use audio or video recording devices to capture their voices and expressions. These interviews provide invaluable firsthand accounts and personal perspectives that add depth to the family history.

Involving other family members in the process of documenting family history is encouraged. They can contribute their own photos, stories, and memories, strengthening family bonds and ensuring a more comprehensive and diverse collection of family history. Consider how you want to share and preserve the documented family history. This can include creating physical or digital albums, publishing a family history book, or sharing the information on a dedicated family website or blog. Ensure that future generations have access to this valuable resource. Remember, documenting family history is a journey that requires time, patience, and ongoing effort. By collating photos, stories, and anecdotes, using online resources, conducting interviews, and engaging family members, retirees can create a rich and meaningful family history cherished by future generations.

In this chapter, you learned about the many amazing ways to keep enriching your family and romantic relationships in retirement. Perhaps you feared that retirement would be isolating and that you'd no longer spend as much time with friends and family as you'd want. However, there are many ways for you to stay connected to your friends and family. In the next chapter, you'll learn more about taking your enjoyment to the next level and embracing your wanderlust.

Chapter 8:

Travel and Exploration

You can make the most of your retirement by fulfilling your travel dreams. Take advantage of travel deals and be open to spontaneous adventures, exploring destinations that have always captured your imagination. Without the constraints of work schedules or limited vacation time, you have the freedom to indulge in your passion for travel.

Start by creating a bucket list that outlines your dream destinations and experiences. Consider the places you've always wanted to visit, whether it's iconic landmarks, natural wonders, or cultural hotspots. Think about the activities and experiences that you love such as hiking in the mountains, exploring historical sites, or immersing yourself in local cuisine.

When planning your travels, consider the physical and mental abilities required for each destination. Choose trips that will be manageable and enjoyable for you. Take into account factors like altitude, climate, and physical exertion. This will ensure that you can fully experience and appreciate each destination without compromising your well-being. Setting a timeline for your travel goals can help you prioritize and plan accordingly. Consider the destinations you want to visit in the near future and those that may require more time or resources to reach. By establishing a timeline, you can create a road map for your travel adventures and make sure you don't miss out on any of your dream destinations.

Shhh... It Doesn't Have to Be Expensive!

Travel on a budget by finding affordable accommodation options, using travel rewards programs and senior discounts, and taking advantage of off-season and last-minute deals. Consider cost-effective alternatives like home exchange programs. Be resourceful and plan ahead to make the most of your travel experiences without breaking the bank. You can also consider travel options where the up-front cost includes your accommodations, meals and some excursions. Also, use a travel agent to help with all aspects of travel and costs.

Discover the benefits of solo travel for personal growth, self-discovery, and the freedom to create your own itineraries. Take safety precautions, stay connected with loved ones, and be mindful of personal limitations while traveling alone.

When planning your retirement travels, don't overlook the local and regional destinations that may be right on your doorstep. Often, interesting and fun places nearby are just waiting for you to find them. Consider enjoying short trips such as biking or walking tours, engaging in geocaching adventures, taking bus or train trips to nearby towns, visiting local art galleries or exhibitions, joining guided tours, or simply spending quality time with friends and family. Another option to consider is renting or buying a trailer or motor home, allowing you to explore your region at your own pace.

Group travel and organized tours can offer unique advantages and experiences. By joining a group tour, you have the convenience of all the logistics and planning taken care of for you. Additionally, you'll have the opportunity to meet like-minded travelers who share your passion for new experiences. Group travel provides a sense of security and companionship, allowing you to focus on enjoying the curated experiences and creating lasting memories.

For those seeking adventure and active travel experiences, you can enjoy plenty of thrilling activities. Consider hiking scenic trails, biking along picturesque routes, embarking on wildlife safaris to observe exotic animals or trying out water sports like kayaking or snorkeling. You could rent a yacht for a day of sailing, or even camp under the stars. Engaging in cultural and educational experiences can greatly enhance your travels. Take the opportunity to visit historical sites, immerse yourself in local festivals and traditions, and participate in workshops or classes that teach you about local crafts or cuisine. These experiences not only enrich your journey but also provide opportunities for learning and personal growth. They foster a deeper understanding of different cultures and allow you to connect with the places you visit on a more meaningful level.

Consider making a positive impact through volunteer and philanthropic travel. By contributing your skills and time to meaningful projects, you can immerse yourself in local communities and make a difference in the lives of others. Engage in activities such as teaching, providing health care support, participating in environmental conservation efforts, or contributing to community development projects. This type of travel allows you to give back while also gaining a deeper appreciation for the local culture and people.

Mind Your Health and Safety!

When traveling during retirement, prioritize safety and health considerations. One important aspect is obtaining travel insurance that can provide coverage for unexpected events such as trip cancellations, medical emergencies, or lost luggage. Review different insurance options and choose a policy that suits your needs and destination.

Depending on where you're going, you may need to get specific vaccinations or take preventive medications. Research the health requirements for your chosen location and consult with a health care professional or travel clinic to ensure you are up-to-date on necessary vaccinations and have any required medications.

If you take regular medications, make sure you have an ample supply for the duration of your trip. Pack medications in your carry-on luggage to ensure they are easily accessible. It's also a good idea to carry a copy of your prescriptions and a list of your medications, including generic names, in case of any emergencies or if you need to refill prescriptions while traveling.

Visiting different climates and environments can have an impact on your health. Be prepared by packing appropriate clothing and accessories to protect yourself from extreme temperatures, sun exposure, or insect bites. Stay hydrated, use sunscreen, and follow any local health guidelines to ensure your well-being.

Before traveling, conduct thorough research about your destination. Familiarize yourself with local customs, laws, and potential health risks. Stay informed about any travel advisories or safety concerns issued by your government or reputable travel sources. This will help you make informed decisions and be prepared for potential challenges.

If you have any specific health concerns or conditions, consult with health care professionals before traveling. They can provide personalized advice, recommend necessary precautions, and address any questions or concerns you may have.

Despite careful planning, unexpected challenges may arise during your travels. Approach these challenges with resilience and adaptability. Stay calm, seek assistance when needed, and be open to alternative solutions. Having a positive mindset and being prepared to navigate unforeseen circumstances will help ensure a smoother travel experience.

Remember, prioritizing travel safety and health considerations is essential for a successful and enjoyable trip. Look for travel insurance, get the necessary vaccinations, and manage your medications. Conduct thorough research so you can be flexible and adapt to different climates and environments. Seek advice from health care professionals before you go so you can minimize potential risks and maximize your travel experience.

Make the Most of Your Journey

Travel and explore in retirement to satisfy your wanderlust, create lasting memories, and continue to grow and learn. Whether it's ticking off destinations from your bucket list, traveling sustainably, exploring local gems, or engaging in adventure and cultural experiences, retirement offers the time and freedom to embark on new adventures. With careful planning, consideration of health and safety, and a sense of curiosity, your travel experiences can create a fulfilling retirement life.

To make the most of your travel experiences, here are some final tips:

- Research and plan. Before embarking on your journey, research your chosen destinations thoroughly. Learn about the local culture, customs, and attractions. Plan your itinerary to make the most of your time and ensure you don't miss out on any must-see sights or experiences.

- Be flexible. While having a plan is important, be open to spontaneity and unexpected opportunities. Leave room for serendipitous discoveries and be willing to deviate from your original itinerary if something exciting comes your way.

- Pack wisely. Pack light and smart. Consider the climate and activities of your destination and pack accordingly. Don't forget essentials like comfortable walking shoes, appropriate clothing, and any necessary medications or documents.

- Immerse yourself in the local culture. Engage with the local community, try local cuisine, and participate in cultural activities. This will enrich your travel experience and create lasting memories.

In this chapter, you learned that travel can be much easier, affordable and exciting than you thought. All you need to do is look into the destinations you're interested in, and then look for the offering that's most friendly to retirees. You can enjoy budget-friendly travel if you carefully account for all the expenses. Immerse yourself in the discovery of new countries and cultures, and don't forget those magnificent local landmarks that you may not have seen.

Yet, travel is only one facet of staying connected and finding fulfillment and purpose. In the next chapter, you will learn how to connect without having to go far by engaging within your own community.

Chapter 9:

Volunteering and Giving

Back

Retirement opens up a world of possibilities! It's a chance to embark on new adventures and make a difference in your community. Volunteering and giving back can bring immense fun and fulfillment during this exciting phase of life. It not only gives you a sense of purpose but also helps you forge meaningful connections and experience personal growth. However, volunteering doesn't only have to include professional skills. You can donate time and effort and offer physical labor to help those in need with various projects and day-to-day activities. You can also give empathy and care to those who are going through hardships. In the following section, you'll explore the significance of volunteering and learn valuable tips for entering this wonderful chapter of retirement.

Embrace the Pathway to Purposeful Engagement

Discover the incredible power of volunteering as you channel your time, skills, and experiences toward making a profound difference in the lives of others. Experience a renewed sense of purpose and fulfillment as you stay active, engaged, and connected to your community. Join the vibrant community of seniors and retirees who are making a positive impact through volunteering.

Start by reflecting on your passions and interests to identify causes or organizations that align with your values and interests. You can begin by volunteering for a few hours a week to gauge your interest and commitment level. Seek opportunities that match your skills, leveraging your professional expertise or hobbies to contribute effectively. Explore various types of volunteering such as mentoring, tutoring, fundraising, or providing administrative support. Or consider joining volunteer groups or organizations to meet people who share similar interests and goals.

Gather information by exploring various volunteer opportunities or organizations, and their positive impact on the community. Set realistic expectations by recognizing your limits and committing to a schedule that aligns with your availability and energy level. Communicate openly with volunteer coordinators, sharing your interests, skills, and availability to discover the perfect match. Seize the chance to try new roles or tasks that can push your abilities and expand your horizons. Celebrate milestones and cherish the meaningful impact you make through your volunteer work.

However, be mindful of your time and energy limitations to avoid overcommitting, and strive for a balance while making a difference. Prioritize your physical and mental well-being to sustain your positive impact as a volunteer. If you ever need guidance or assistance, feel free to reach out to volunteer coordinators or your fellow volunteers; they're there to support you. Keep in mind that the impact of your volunteer work may not be immediate, so stay patient and know that your efforts will make a difference in the long run.

Where to Volunteer?

When you think about volunteering, your mind probably goes to the more common opportunities: food banks, animal shelters, schools, hospitals, hospices, or environmental organizations. However, many other types of organizations need help, and you have many ways to find them. When looking, think about their impact, values, and location, and the type of help they need.

Support Nonprofit Organizations

Learn about the variety of nonprofit organizations that rely on volunteers. Consider contributing your time and expertise through board membership or leadership roles. Taking on these positions, allows you to directly impact the organization's mission and help shape its future. You'll have the opportunity to work closely with other passionate people who share your commitment to making a difference. Additionally, a leadership role can provide valuable personal and professional growth opportunities, and help you to develop new skills. It can also lead to more involvement in the nonprofit sector, further boosting your growth and impact.

Use Your Professional Expertise

Offer your professional skills to assist nonprofits or mentor younger professionals. Skills-based volunteering can be a valuable way to make a meaningful impact. Your expertise may allow you to lend specialized support to nonprofit organizations. These organizations may not have the resources to hire professional counsel, consultancy, or talent. Whether you're offering legal advice, manual labor, marketing assistance, seasoned experience, or financial expertise, your professional skills could make a significant difference in helping nonprofits achieve their goals. Mentoring younger professionals can be rewarding, as you get to guide and inspire the next generation of nonprofit sector leaders.

Explore International Volunteering

Consider participating in global humanitarian projects or joining international organizations to make a difference on an international scale. Research options like Seniors Volunteer Abroad, Volunteer World, Projects Abroad, and Go Eco. These organizations provide opportunities to do charitable and philanthropic work around the globe. You also get to experience different cultures and communities, and gain a new perspective on global issues. Aside from contributing to sustainable development or other efforts, international volunteering helps you connect with philanthropists from diverse backgrounds. Volunteering and charitable work in other countries can help build international rapport and promote cross-cultural understanding and collaboration.

Embrace Virtual Volunteering

Take advantage of the rise in virtual volunteering opportunities. Contribute remotely through online tutoring, virtual mentoring, helping with administrative tasks, or any number of other ways. You can make a difference by lending your expertise from the comfort of your own home. Virtual volunteering is flexible and convenient, allowing you to work on your schedule. Even if you only have a few hours a week to spare, many organizations and platforms that require remote or online assistance will love to have you on board. Using your skills and knowledge online in this way is a chance to support causes and communities across the globe without having to sacrifice more of your time and energy than you have.

Volunteer for Seniors

Explore opportunities in programs and organizations that support and assist seniors, such as elder care facilities, senior centers, or programs focused on reducing social isolation. With the aging population growing, the need for support and companionship for seniors grows as well. You can volunteer to help out other seniors and keep them company, and in this way, make a meaningful impact on their lives. Whether it's organizing and planning, providing companionship, or helping out with daily tasks, your time and presence can truly help other seniors live better-quality lives. At the same time, you also get to enjoy new friendships and forge meaningful connections.

Support Environmental Crisis Causes

Contribute to environmental conservation by getting involved in activities that make a positive impact. You can participate in citizen science programs, engage in environmental education, help with trail maintenance, contribute to habitat restoration, support environmental advocacy, join community gardening initiatives, or even assist with wildlife rehabilitation. It's a wonderful way for you to make a difference and be part of something meaningful. Consider training and volunteering with organizations involved in providing aid during crises. Your experience and skills can be incredibly valuable in times of emergency. You have the power to make a difference and help those in need when disaster strikes.

Become a Mentor

Embrace mentoring and share your expertise to make a positive difference in the lives of young people. Mentoring has been shown to improve cognitive functioning and bring fun to both you and the mentees. Why not explore opportunities like mentoring fatherless boys or listening to kids read? It's a wonderful way to spread warmth and uplift others!

In this chapter, you learned that volunteering and giving back during retirement can help you discover a newfound sense of purpose, fulfillment, and the fun of making a positive impact. You can get involved in your local community, support nonprofit organizations, or use your skills to help others. Other opportunities include participating in international or virtual projects or becoming a mentor. You can contribute your time, skills, and expertise in countless ways for the betterment of society.

Chapter 10:

Learning and Growing

Retirement is an incredible chapter of your life that presents the chance for personal growth, intellectual development, and a truly fulfilling lifestyle. Embrace a mindset of lifelong learning to keep expanding your knowledge, exploring new interests, and staying mentally engaged.

Lifelong Learning Mindset

New challenges and experiences can push you out of your comfort zone. So as you start this exciting journey, don't be afraid to take some risks. Also, get involved in discussions and share your valuable insights with other learners. Connect with fellow retirees who are on the same path as you and exchange ideas, thoughts, and perspectives. By doing this, you can create a lively and supportive learning community. Make sure to set realistic goals for your learning journey and celebrate your achievements along the way. Take the time to define your goals and break them down into manageable steps. And as you make progress, remember to celebrate each milestone, big or small.

As you start your learning journey, try new and exciting topics. Don't worry if you face challenges or setbacks at first. Learning takes time, so believe in yourself and keep going.

Pursue Formal Education

Take a chance and explore the variety of options you have to expand your knowledge and skills. Whether you're interested in pursuing a degree, diploma, or certificate, or simply taking college courses, the world of learning is open to you. You can enhance your existing skills and find new interests through continuing education and professional development opportunities. Take advantage of workshops, seminars, and online courses to further enrich your learning experience. The possibilities are endless, and the fun of learning awaits you!

To get started, consider enrolling in degree or certificate programs that align with your interests or aspirations. Plenty of online courses and platforms offer flexibility and convenience, allowing you to learn at your own pace. Don't forget to look for scholarships or discounts available specifically for retirees pursuing formal education.

Embark on your educational adventure by being wise and organized. First, create a study schedule and make sure to set aside dedicated time for your learning journey. Remember, consistency is key! Next, don't hesitate to engage with professors, instructors, and fellow students. Building connections and actively participating in discussions will enhance your learning experience—and benefit others in the class as well. Lastly, make the most of the resources available to you. Libraries, research databases, and academic support services are there to support your growth. So, seize the opportunity and let these resources guide you toward success!

When it comes to pursuing your dreams, remember a few key things. First, don't feel pressured to pursue formal education if that isn't what you want to do. Instead, follow your passions and explore what truly excites you. Second, avoid overwhelming yourself with too many courses or commitments. Find a balance that suits your lifestyle and learning capacity. Remember, this is your journey, and you have the power to shape it in a way that brings you fun and fulfillment. So go ahead, embrace your passions, and create a path that's uniquely yours!

Book Clubs and Literary Circles

Joining book clubs and literary circles can be amazing ways to engage in meaningful discussions, expand your literary horizons, and connect with fellow book enthusiasts. These groups provide platforms for intellectual stimulation, social interaction, and the exploration of diverse perspectives. Research local book clubs or literary circles that cater to retirees or specific genres you're interested in, and actively participate in discussions by sharing your thoughts and insights. If there are no book clubs in your area, consider starting your own.

To broaden your literary knowledge, read a variety of genres and authors, and attend author readings, literary festivals, or book-related events. Foster a welcoming and inclusive environment within the book club, encouraging diverse opinions and perspectives. Embrace the opportunity to explore different literary styles instead of limiting yourself to familiar genres or authors. Remember to engage in respectful dialogue and remain open-minded, avoiding the domination of discussions or dismissal of others' viewpoints.

Personal Development Workshops

Personal development workshops and seminars offer retirees incredible opportunities to enhance various aspects of their lives. By diving into topics such as communication skills, leadership development, mindfulness, and emotional intelligence, you can support your personal growth and self-improvement. To get started, research local organizations, community centers, or online platforms that offer tailored workshops for retirees.

Consider attending retreats or immersive programs for a deeper exploration of personal development topics. Approach these workshops with an open mind and a genuine desire to learn and grow. Engage actively in discussions, exercises, and activities to make the most of your learning experience. Apply the knowledge and skills you gain to your daily life and relationships. Don't feel overwhelmed by the abundance of workshops available. Choose the ones that fit your personal goals and interests. Remember, personal development is a continuous journey that requires patience and practice. Now that you really have the time, embrace these exciting opportunities. The possibilities are endless!

Creative and Artistic Expression

Retirement offers an ideal opportunity to pursue creative and artistic endeavors such as painting, writing, music, or crafts, allowing for self-expression, self-discovery, and continuous learning. To maximize this time, consider the following tips:

- Create a dedicated space or studio for your creative pursuits. Find one or more spots in your home, front yard, or back yard that seem perfect for creativity. These spots should have enough space and light, and a pleasant view to naturally inspire creativity. They should also provide a bit of solitude and isolation when needed so that you can work in peace.

- Attend local art classes, writing workshops, or music lessons to enhance your skills. Taking classes may help you see that you can learn a lot more than you thought you could. The phrase "it's never too late" has never been more accurate than in retirement. You can take up any skill or hobby you want and spend the time and effort you need to get the hang of it.

- Connect with fellow creatives by joining art groups, writing circles, or music ensembles. You can exchange project ideas and tips for practical work, advise on best supplies and hacks, and so much more.

- Explore various mediums, styles, or genres to uncover your preferences. Nowadays, learning has become highly personalized. For example, if you think about painting, your first association might be oil painting on large canvases with clunky brushes and heavily scented paints. If this is not for you, guess what? You can paint watercolor miniatures. You can adjust any art or craft to accommodate your personality, preferences, and needs.

- Share your creative work through exhibitions, readings, or performances. Don't be ashamed of your artistic works. Nobody expects them to be perfect, but your friends and family will adore them because they are yours, made with a lot of effort, inspiration, and love.

Finally, embrace the creative process without judgment or self-criticism. Avoid comparing your work to other people's. Focus instead on your own growth and enjoyment, and on not allowing initial challenges or setbacks to discourage you. Creativity requires practice and perseverance.

Personal Reflection and Journaling

Encourage yourself to engage in personal reflection and journaling to discover more about yourself, express your thoughts, and capture precious memories and life experiences. Writing can be a therapeutic and introspective activity that promotes personal growth and mindfulness. To enhance your journaling experience, consider the following tips:

- Set aside dedicated time for personal reflection and journaling. You don't need a ton of time for writing. You can dedicate anywhere from five minutes to several hours to journaling and other mindfulness routines, if you're up for it.

- Experiment with different techniques, such as gratitude journaling or free writing. If you don't enjoy writing or you struggle with it, you can record your thoughts on your mobile device and listen to them later on.

- Consider joining writing groups or workshops that focus on personal narratives or memoir writing. Documenting your life journey may look like a massive undertaking, but it can help you round up your experiences and leave them as a legacy to your loved ones. The technique for doing this can be tricky. This is where classes and study groups come in to help you find the right way.

- Write without judgment or self-censorship, allowing your thoughts and emotions to flow freely. Being accepting and nonjudgmental when recording your thoughts and feelings helps you process them completely, leaving no regrets behind.

- Use journaling as a tool for self-reflection, exploring your values, goals, and dreams. Reflecting on the essence of who you are is deeply relaxing and refreshing. It can help you process major life changes and intense feelings.

- Revisit your journal entries periodically to gain insights and track your personal growth.

To make the most of your journaling practice, remember that you're not obligated to write every day or meet specific word counts. Journaling should be a personal and flexible practice. Avoid comparing your journaling style or content to others. Embrace your unique voice and experiences.

Wellness and Mind-Body Practices

Engaging in wellness and mind-body practices such as meditation, mindfulness, yoga, or tai chi can bring incredible health benefits and positively impact your personal growth. These practices help you relax, reduce stress, and connect with yourself on a deeper level.

To get started, look for local wellness centers, community classes, or online platforms that offer mind-body practices. Begin with short meditations or mindfulness sessions and gradually increase the duration as you feel more comfortable. Consider attending workshops or retreats that provide guidance and a deeper immersion into these practices. Remember to establish a regular routine that fits your schedule. Approach mind-body practices with an open mind, ready to explore different techniques. Be patient with yourself and allow the benefits of these practices to unfold gradually. Avoid expecting immediate results or perfection. It's a continuous journey of self-discovery. Also, avoid comparing your practice to other people's. Your experience is unique and personal.

Digital Literacy and Technology Skills

Recognizing the importance of digital literacy and technology skills in retirement, let's explore the world of smartphones, tablets, social media, and other digital tools. These resources can help you stay connected, learn, and access information. To start, consider attending local technology classes or workshops specifically designed for retirees. These sessions allow you to learn at your own pace. Don't hesitate to seek assistance from family, friends, or community organizations. They can guide you through the basics of digital skills. You can also explore online tutorials and resources that offer step-by-step guidance. These valuable tools will help you navigate the digital world with ease.

When getting started, focus on the fundamentals such as email, internet browsing, and social media. These skills will open up a whole new world of possibilities. As you become more comfortable, gradually explore more advanced features and applications that align with your interests and needs. Stay up to date with the latest technology trends and security practices to ensure a safe digital experience.

Technology can seem overwhelming, but you can take it one step at a time. Focus on what matters to you. If you encounter challenges or difficulties, don't hesitate to ask for help or seek additional resources. Support is always available. Embrace technology and enjoy the digital adventure that can bring joy, connection, and endless opportunities.

Supportive Learning Networks

Encourage yourself to actively engage in supportive learning networks such as discussion groups, online forums, study circles, or social clubs. These networks provide intellectual stimulation, an exchange of ideas, and the opportunity to create meaningful connections. Join local community groups or organizations that focus on specific areas of interest.

Explore online forums or social media groups dedicated to retirees or specific topics. Attend conferences, seminars, or events that bring together individuals with similar passions or interests. Participate actively in discussions, sharing your knowledge and insights. Foster a supportive and inclusive environment within the learning network. Seek opportunities for collaboration, joint projects, or shared learning experiences. Don't limit yourself to familiar networks or groups. Embrace the opportunity to connect with people from diverse backgrounds and perspectives. Don't shy away from sharing your thoughts or ideas. Your contributions are valuable and can inspire others.

Leading a happy and fulfilling life in retirement involves embracing a lifelong learning mindset and actively engaging in various opportunities for personal growth and intellectual development. By pursuing formal education, joining book clubs, exploring new hobbies, attending personal development workshops, or engaging in creative expression, you can continue to learn, grow, and thrive in this new chapter of life. Or you could try practicing personal reflection, embracing wellness activities, developing digital literacy, and participating in supportive learning networks. Whichever way you go, you'll find your retirement years more enriching.

In this chapter, you learned that retirement is the perfect time for you to get into the groove of lifelong learning. It's a chance to grow personally, keep your mind sharp, and try new things. By staying curious and open-minded, you can keep expanding your knowledge and skills, making your retirement even more awesome. Check out local community programs and resources that are all about education for retirees. They've got a lot for you to explore and learn from. And don't forget about online learning platforms where you can find a wide range of subjects and courses just for you, all at your fingertips. Lectures, workshops, and seminars are available to match your interests and needs, no matter what you're seeking. With these opportunities, you can keep growing and learning, and loving your retirement years.

Chapter 11:

Leisure and Hobbies

Retirement is your opportunity to enjoy leisure activities, discover new hobbies, and cultivate a fulfilling lifestyle. Engaging in these activities will not only bring you enjoyment but also promote personal growth, social connection, and overall well-being. Let's explore various aspects of living a leisurely and fulfilling life in retirement!

Leisure Activities and New Hobbies

Leisure activities and hobbies can be your ticket to a fulfilling retirement, offering joy, personal growth, and endless possibilities. To start, reflect on your interests and past hobbies. Maybe it's time to try something new or get back into an old hobby. Stepping out of your comfort zone and taking on new experiences can be invigorating. Allocate dedicated time for your chosen activities and embrace a spirit of adventure and curiosity. Remember to prioritize enjoyment and personal growth in your leisure pursuits. Don't limit yourself or feel pressured to excel. Instead, enjoy the freedom to try new things and discover joy.

Gym, Fitness, and Sports

Physical fitness and sports offer a multitude of benefits, and promote health, strength, and vitality—not to mention providing opportunities for social interaction. Try golfing, bowling, walking or other group activities that allow you to exercise, have fun, and socialize. Choose activities that match your fitness level, whether it's low-impact exercises, group classes, or sports you enjoy.

Set realistic goals, track your progress, and experience a wonderful sense of accomplishment along the way. Remember to consult with health care professionals before starting any new fitness or sports activities. Prioritize warm-up and cool-down routines, listen to your body, and rest when needed. Respect your body's capabilities, avoid overexertion, and don't compare yourself to others. Focus on your own progress, recognize your achievements, and celebrate the milestones you reach. Keep going. Every step you take gets you closer to a healthier and happier you!

Outdoor Recreation and Exploration

Once you've retired, you probably have more time to get outside and enjoy nature, stay active, and embark on exciting adventures. Immerse yourself in the beauty of the natural world while hiking, biking, fishing, bird watching, or geocaching. Researching local outdoor destinations uncovers nearby parks, trails, or natural areas that offer fantastic opportunities for outdoor recreation. Investing in appropriate gear ensures you have all the necessary equipment and attire to get outside safely and comfortably. Group activities may enhance your outdoor experience. Joining outdoor clubs or organizations fosters social connections and creates shared experiences. So get out there, explore, and embrace the wonders of the great outdoors!

To make the most of your outdoor adventures, prioritize safety. Familiarize yourself with safety guidelines and precautions for each activity. Stay hydrated, protect yourself from the elements, and be aware of your surroundings. Respect the environment by practicing responsible outdoor ethics. Leave no trace, show respect for wildlife, and stick to designated trails. Doing so preserves the beauty of nature for future generations to enjoy.

When it comes to outdoor activities, do not underestimate the difficulty level. Choose activities that match your fitness level and abilities. Begin with easier trails or activities and gradually progress as you build strength and endurance. Planning ahead is key! Inform someone about your plans, pack all the necessary supplies, and be prepared for any unexpected changes in weather or conditions. Stay safe and enjoy your outdoor adventures!

Travel and Exploration

Traveling and exploring new destinations can be an exciting and fulfilling adventure for you in retirement. It's a chance to immerse yourself in different cultures, create unforgettable memories, and expand your horizons. Here are some tips to make the most of your travel experiences:

- Plan ahead by researching destinations, creating itineraries, and considering factors like budget, accessibility, and personal interests.

- Consider group travel as a fantastic opportunity to meet new people, forge connections, and enjoy a supportive and social experience.

- Embrace the concept of slow travel, immersing yourself in the local culture, savoring flavors, and soaking in the unique atmosphere of each destination.

- Embrace spontaneity, leave room for unexpected discoveries, and be open to new opportunities.

- Document your adventures with a travel journal and photographs, preserving precious memories.

- Pace yourself, take breaks, and prioritize relaxation.

- Explore your own region or country for hidden gems and unique experiences.

Get ready to embark on incredible adventures, make new friends, and create lifelong memories as you explore the world in retirement!

Creative and Artistic Expression

Engaging in creative and artistic activities during retirement provides a wonderful opportunity for self-expression, personal fulfillment, and tapping into creativity. Whether it's writing, photography, knitting, woodworking, or any other artistic pursuit, these activities can bring immense fulfillment and a sense of accomplishment.

Start with what interests you. Take classes or workshops to further fuel your creative fire and enhance your skills. Share your work with the world—display your paintings, share your writing, or participate in art exhibitions and craft fairs. Embrace the importance of creation and express yourself. Experiment with and explore different artistic mediums and techniques. Join creative communities and connect with other artists, writers, or crafters. Focus on the process and enjoy the journey of creating. View imperfections as part of the creative process. Don't compare yourself to others. Embrace your own creativity without worrying about how it measures up.

Reading and Book Clubs

Reading brings joy, relaxation, and the opportunity for exciting adventures. Enhance your reading experience by joining book clubs or discussion groups to connect with fellow book lovers and share insights. There are plenty of ways to make your reading journey fulfilling. You can expand your literary horizons by exploring books from various genres. Step out of your comfort zone and discover new favorites. Consider joining local book clubs or online communities aligned with your interests. Engage in discussions, sharing your thoughts, and listening to others' perspectives. To enhance your reading experience, dedicate time in your schedule. Find a cozy space to immerse yourself in books. Don't feel obligated to finish every book. Set aside those that don't grab you.

If you're in a group, listen to diverse viewpoints and engage in respectful conversations. Create a warm and welcoming environment for seniors or retirees to enjoy the journey that books offer. Share your thoughts and opinions in book club discussions. Contribute to the conversation and spark exchanges with fellow readers. Let's make the book club vibrant and engaging for everyone!

Pursuing Part-Time Hobbies and Crafts

Retirement offers the perfect chance to embrace part-time hobbies or crafts that may have taken a back seat while you were working. Do you miss the joy, fulfillment, and wonderful sense of accomplishment they used to bring? Rekindle your love for activities you enjoyed in the past like painting, gardening, playing a musical instrument, or cooking.

Explore new interests and let your curiosity guide you. Join clubs or groups focused on your chosen hobby or craft for a sense of community and exciting collaboration. Set realistic goals, break down tasks, and consider teaching or mentoring others. Make sure to set aside dedicated time and invest in necessary resources. Seek inspiration, connect with fellow enthusiasts, and embrace your creativity.

Avoid comparing yourself to others. Don't let setbacks discourage you. Be fearless in trying new things and don't let perfectionism hinder your enjoyment. By partaking in hobbies or crafts, you can find purpose, fulfillment, and a renewed sense of self during retirement. Cultural and artistic activities provide opportunities to appreciate and actively participate in the arts. Join a community theater or music or choir groups, and attend concerts, theater performances, or art exhibitions to deepen your connection with the arts.

Stay informed about upcoming concerts, theater performances, art exhibitions, and community events in your area by researching local cultural events. Discover a world of entertainment and creativity right at your fingertips. Consider taking classes or workshops on acting, singing, painting, or other artistic disciplines you've always wanted to try. Unleash your inner artist and let your creativity soar!

If you're looking for a meaningful way to give back, offer your time and expertise to support local cultural organizations. By volunteering, you not only gain behind-the-scenes experiences but also contribute to the arts community. Your passion and dedication can make a real difference. Embrace the arts, dear reader! Immerse yourself in the magic of live performances, explore your artistic talents, and become an integral part of your local cultural scene. The possibilities are endless, and the fulfillment you'll experience is simply priceless.

Let cultural events captivate your senses! Open your mind and allow yourself to be moved and inspired by the artistic performances or exhibitions that unfold before you. Engage with the artists, performers, or curators. Ask them questions, share your thoughts, and express your heartfelt appreciation for their incredible work. It's through these interactions that you'll truly deepen your connection to the vibrant world of art and culture. Embrace the magic and let your spirit soar!

Don't limit yourself to familiar art forms—expand your artistic horizons by exploring new genres and styles. Embrace new experiences and discover the importance of different artistic expressions. Let your emotions flow freely through art. Allow yourself to feel and respond to the powerful emotions that art can evoke. Let art be a source of inspiration and a way to connect with your inner self.

Collecting

Collecting items of personal interest can bring fulfillment to your retirement years. The thrill lies in the excitement of the hunt, the importance of discovery, and sharing these treasures with others. Here are tips to make your collecting journey more enjoyable:

- Choose a theme you're sure to enjoy. Think about the type of items you can't get enough of, and are willing to invest time, effort, and resources to acquire and maintain.

- Research and educate yourself about the items you collect. Collectibles can have significant value, and many hidden gems are being sold for pennies. Don't let them slip through your fingers!

- Connect with other collectors who share your passion. There's no one better than like-minded collectors to advise you on purchases and maintenance of your beloved trinkets.

- Set goals for yourself and take good care of your collection. Think about the number of items you want and can store, the manner in which you'll store them, and the amount of time and effort that you can dedicate to their upkeep.

- Don't let collecting become overwhelming. Collectibles serve you, and not the other way around. Set your boundaries with collecting to ensure that it doesn't take up too much of your time, space, or money.

- Remember to enjoy the process and share your collection with others. Be proud of your collection, display it thoughtfully in your home, take pictures, and share your passion with other enthusiasts. After all, you also will have valuable knowledge to share after collecting for a while.

Happy collecting and may your retirement years be filled with treasure hunts and cherished memories!

Cooking and Culinary Exploration

Cooking and exploring the culinary world can add real flavor to your retirement. Trying new recipes, attending cooking classes, and hosting dinner parties allows you to unleash creativity, experiment with flavors, and savor delicious meals. Look into different cuisines, experiment with recipes from various cultures, and broaden your culinary horizons.

You can expand your culinary horizons in many ways. Join cooking classes or workshops to enhance your skills and learn and grow as a home chef. Share your creations by hosting dinner parties or potluck gatherings, bringing people together, and creating unforgettable experiences. Embrace culinary experimentation by trying new ingredients, techniques, and recipes. Document your favorite recipes in a personal collection or journal to preserve memories. Don't be afraid to make mistakes; they are opportunities for growth. Explore different cuisines and flavors, allowing yourself to discover new favorites. Enjoy your culinary adventures and have a fantastic time exploring the world of flavors and tastes!

Gaming and Puzzle-Solving

Gaming and puzzle-solving during retirement provides mental stimulation, entertainment, and opportunities for social connection. Whether you enjoy chess, bridge, crossword puzzles, sudoku, or video games, these activities keep your mind sharp and foster social interaction.

When you're choosing games, look for ones you can play at your desired level of challenge. Join gaming or puzzle groups to connect with others who share your passion. Find these groups through local clubs, online communities, or organized events. Explore online gaming platforms or puzzle-solving apps like Solitaire and Wordle for a wide range of entertainment. You could also consider jigsaw puzzles, bingo, cards, board games, chess, and many other activities.

Prioritize balance in retirement by enjoying gaming and puzzles in moderation, complementing other aspects of your lifestyle. Engage in multiplayer games for social interaction and friendly competition. Don't forget to make time for physical activity, socializing, and pursuing personal hobbies. Embrace the mental stimulation and problem-solving nature of gaming and puzzles, viewing challenges as exciting opportunities for growth and improvement.

Living a happy and fulfilling life in retirement means embracing leisure activities, exploring new hobbies, and engaging in various pursuits that bring you joy, personal growth, and social connection. Embrace novelty and stay physically fit so you can explore the outdoors and travel. Express your creativity, read, participate in cultural events, collect, cook, and enjoy gaming and puzzles to create a fulfilling retirement lifestyle. Remember to prioritize enjoyment, personal growth, and social connections as you embark on this exciting chapter of life.

Chapter 12:

Estate Planning

Estate planning is a vital part of your retirement journey. It allows you to make decisions regarding your assets, end-of-life matters, and how you'll take care of your loved ones. Let's look at how estate planning can bring efficiency and peace of mind to your life! Estate planning empowers you to maintain control over your assets, safeguard your loved ones, and ensure that your desires are honored. It minimizes potential conflicts, and facilitates a seamless transfer of wealth and personal belongings.

Seeking professional guidance is essential for a smooth retirement journey. Enlist the support of a seasoned estate planning attorney or financial advisor who specializes in retirement planning. They have the expertise to offer valuable guidance and help you create a comprehensive and effective plan. With their help, you can move forward confidently and make informed decisions that will benefit you in the long run.

Will and Testament

Crafting a legally binding will is essential for you. It allows you to clearly outline the distribution of your assets, designate beneficiaries, and address unique circumstances that may arise. These circumstances could include blended families, stepchildren, ex-spouses, or guardianship of dependents, elderly parents, or individuals with special needs. Remember to review and update your will regularly to ensure it reflects any changes in your personal situation or family dynamics. By doing so, you can have peace of mind knowing that your wishes are protected and your loved ones are taken care of.

Power of Attorney

Appointing a trusted individual as your power of attorney is a smart move. This person will have the authority to make financial or health care decisions on your behalf if you ever can't do it yourself. Choose someone who truly understands your wishes and values. Make sure they are not only willing but also capable of fulfilling this important role. By doing so, you'll know that your interests will be taken care of, even in challenging times.

Potential Health Care Directives

To ensure you have control over your potential medical decisions and end-of-life care preferences, you can create health care directives. Start by drafting a living will or appointing a health care proxy who can advocate for your wishes. This lets you know that your voice will be heard when it matters most.

In addition to health care directives, it's wise to explore options for potential long-term health care needs. Consider looking into long-term care insurance that can provide financial support for any future care you may require. It's also a good idea to set aside funds specifically for medical expenses, ensuring that you're prepared for any unexpected health care costs that may arise. By taking these proactive steps, you're empowering yourself to make informed decisions about your health and well-being.

Remember, it's never too early to plan for the future and prioritize your own care. You can also explore the benefits of establishing trusts—such as revocable living trusts or irrevocable trusts—to protect your assets, minimize estate taxes, and ensure the efficient transfer of wealth. Seek professional advice to determine the most suitable type of trust for your specific circumstances.

Taxes and Business Succession

Consider strategies to minimize your tax liabilities, including gifting strategies, asset valuation techniques, and utilizing tax exemptions available in your country or state of residence. Stay informed about changes in tax laws and consult with a tax professional to ensure compliance and optimize tax planning.

If you own a business, plan for its succession or cessation by considering potential successors, establishing buy-sell agreements, or setting up trusts to ensure a smooth transition. Seek legal and financial advice to develop a comprehensive business succession plan.

You can also consider including charitable giving in your estate planning by setting up charitable trusts, donor-advised funds, or leaving bequests to charitable organizations. Discuss your philanthropic goals with a financial advisor or attorney to determine the most effective ways to support causes you care about.

Digital Estate Planning

Address the importance of recording or designating your digital assets, passwords, and instructions for online accounts, bank accounts, and insurance to ensure ease of management and access after your passing. Consider using password managers or digital estate planning services to securely store and share this information.

Decluttering

Take the time to declutter and organize your belongings, identifying items of family or emotional significance and expressing your wishes for their distribution. Eliminate unnecessary items to reduce the burden on loved ones and make the process of asset distribution more manageable.

Regular Review and Updates

Emphasize the importance of regularly reviewing and updating your estate planning documents, including wills, beneficiaries, accounts, life insurance policies, and other financial assets. Changes in personal circumstances, family dynamics, and legal requirements should be reflected in the estate plan to ensure its accuracy and effectiveness. By addressing these aspects of estate planning, you can ensure your wishes are respected, your loved ones are protected, and the transition of assets is handled efficiently and smoothly. Seeking professional guidance and regularly reviewing and updating your estate plan are key to maintaining its relevance and effectiveness over time.

Potential Long-Term Care Planning

Long-term care planning is a crucial consideration for retirees. It involves preparing for any potential future health care needs and associated costs, ensuring financial security, and accessing quality care. To help you navigate this process, here are some tips:

- Research different long-term care options to gain a better understanding of the available services and associated costs.

- Consider consulting a financial advisor to explore the option of long-term care insurance.

- Plan for potential caregiving needs by discussing them with your loved ones and exploring professional services.

- Review your financial resources, including retirement savings and investments, to ensure they align with your long-term care goals.

- Don't forget to include your long-term care preferences in your health care directives and communicate your wishes to your health care agent and family members.

To help make the process easier on your family and loved ones, consider these planning steps:

- Start planning as early as possible to ensure you have enough resources in place.

- Think about long-term care options and financial planning well before retirement.

- Involve the people around you in the decision-making process to gain their support and understanding.

- Don't underestimate the potential costs associated with long-term care. Make sure you have a realistic understanding of the financial implications and don't assume that Medicare or other insurance will cover everything.

- Avoid delaying planning, as it can limit your options and strain your finances in the future.

Estate planning is an exciting and empowering process that allows you to shape your retirement years with fun and fulfillment. As you embark on this journey, consider various aspects such as creating wills and trusts, establishing powers of attorney, planning for health care directives, and minimizing tax liabilities. Help the ones you leave behind by addressing your business needs and charitable giving, planning for digital assets, and, of course, decluttering. By approaching each aspect with care and seeking professional advice when needed, you can ensure peace of mind, protect your loved ones, and smoothly transition your assets and end-of-life decisions.

Remember to regularly review and update your plans to adapt to changing circumstances. With a solid foundation in place, you can embark on a retirement journey filled with happiness and fulfillment.

End-of-Life Planning

We must emphasize the significance of long-term health care and end-of-life planning. In this section, we'll consider financial and insurance considerations, advanced care directives, health care proxies, and the need for meaningful conversations about your personal values and wishes regarding medical decisions. Here's a breakdown of considerations for end-of-life planning:

- Create advance care directives such as a living will and a health care power of attorney to ensure your medical preferences are known and someone you trust can make decisions for you, if needed.

- Discuss your wishes with loved ones. Have open and honest conversations with your loved ones about your end-of-life wishes. Talk about your preferences for medical treatment, life-sustaining measures, and funeral arrangements. That way, you can make sure that your wishes are known and respected. Make sure to choose a health care proxy. Select someone you trust to make medical decisions for you if you can't. Have a conversation with that person about your values, beliefs, and treatment preferences so they can be your strong advocate.

- Next, consider exploring palliative and hospice care options. Learn about the benefits of palliative care, which focuses on relieving symptoms and enhancing your quality of life if you choose not to treat an illness aggressively. Additionally, hospice care offers comfort and support for people with terminal illnesses. Take the time to understand the available services and talk to your health care provider about them.

- Consider the incredible gift of organ donation and how you can make a difference. You may have the power to be an organ donor and positively impact lives. Share your decision with your loved ones and, if you choose, register as an organ donor.

- Review and update your financial and legal documents, including your will, trusts, and beneficiary designations. Consult with an attorney or financial advisor to make sure your affairs are in order. It's always a good idea to take care of these important matters!

- Consider your preferences for funeral or memorial services, burial, cremation, or other options. Let your loved ones know about your wishes and think about pre-planning or pre-paying for funeral arrangements if it brings you peace of mind. Seek emotional and spiritual support as you embark on your end-of-life planning journey. You can reach out to a counselor, therapist, or religious/spiritual advisor for guidance and comfort to uplift your spirits. Remember, you're not alone in this process!

Reviewing and updating your end-of-life planning documents regularly ensures that they always reflect your current wishes. Remember, life circumstances and preferences can change over time, so it's important to keep these documents up to date. Communicate with your health care providers by sharing your end-of-life plans and documents with them. Make sure they are aware of your wishes and have a copy of your advance care directives on file. It's important to keep the lines of communication open so that everyone is on the same page when it comes to your health care decisions.

End-of-life planning is a sensitive but important journey that allows you to shape your future. Take a moment to ponder your values, share your desires with your loved ones, and seek expert advice whenever you need it. Remember, retirement is an adventure brimming with chances to prioritize your well-being. Embrace it wholeheartedly, nurturing your body, mind, heart, and connections. Just don't forget to prepare for what comes next.

By adopting healthy habits, seeking support when needed, and preparing for long-term care, you can enhance your overall quality of life and relish a retirement experience that is truly fulfilling and harmonious. Addressing personal family matters and making decisions regarding funeral wishes and the distribution of personal possessions are important steps for you. You can share your preferences with your loved ones and consider writing them down in a letter of instruction. This will not only provide guidance but also ease the process for them, ensuring that your wishes are respected and honored.

Remember to start by organizing your assets and planning for the distribution of your estate after you pass away. Consult with an estate planning attorney who will help you create a comprehensive plan tailored to your needs. This plan will include important documents like a will, trusts, and powers of attorney. By having this plan in place, you can ensure that your assets are distributed exactly as you wish them to be. It's a comforting thought, knowing that your hard-earned assets will be taken care of and passed on to your loved ones according to your desires.

Conclusion

Great work! You are now ready to live your Retirement Redefined! Hopefully, this book has shown you that getting ready for retirement is much more about you than it is about finances, estate, and health care. It includes traveling and enjoying leisure and hobbies, along with staying socially engaged. You can enjoy quality time with your family, and focus on all those things that you used to be too busy to do. You can make scrapbooks, have long and meaningful conversations, and live the kind of peaceful, mindful life that you always dreamed about.

The exciting journey of retirement is all about embracing the multitude of opportunities that shape this transformative phase. The redefined retirement that you get to enjoy is now enriched with longevity and opportunities to be creative and productive. You can enjoy the kind of inspired work that you choose. It may be part hobby and part work, or you may entirely donate your skills, effort, and kindness to those in need. With valuable professional experience under your belt, you can further spread your knowledge as a mentor or a coach.

A fulfilling retirement includes many vital pieces: financial considerations, estate planning, legal matters, lifestyle choices, family dynamics, and physical, emotional and psychological well-being. You can find ways to nurture hobbies and indulge in leisure activities. All it takes is thinking and planning ahead.

Among the important aspects, prioritizing estate planning emerges as a crucial cornerstone, ensuring a secure and seamless transition for the future. It helps safeguard your health care and long-term care choices.

Seeking guidance from a financial advisor and an estate planning attorney will help you understand the impact of your choices on your financial plan and ensure adequate insurance coverage. By considering your health and long-term care needs, you'll be better prepared for potential expenses. This will enable you make informed decisions that protect your financial well-being during retirement. To create a solid retirement plan, follow these key steps.

- Envision your ideal retirement lifestyle, then set goals and priorities. This way, you create a clear vision of what you want to achieve during this phase of your life, empowering you to make intentional choices and turn your vision into reality.

- Assess your financial situation by evaluating your savings, investments, and potential sources of income. This review of your assets allows you to calculate your net worth and identify areas that need attention. Consulting with a financial advisor can expand your thinking and help you create a comprehensive retirement plan.

- Develop a realistic budget so you can manage your finances during retirement. This involves identifying expenses and allocating funds accordingly. Additionally, you must consider your desired lifestyle and set aside money for discretionary expenses. By creating a budget, you ensure that you have enough resources to support your retirement lifestyle.

- Explore different retirement savings options so you can make the most of your savings potential. Learn the contribution limits, investment options, and withdrawal rules so you can make informed decisions about where to allocate your savings and how to diversify your investments.

- Make sure your wishes are respected by establishing a power of attorney, a health care proxy, and a living will. These documents take your place if you're unable to make medical decisions. Remember to review and update your documents regularly to keep up with changing needs.

By envisioning your retirement lifestyle, assessing your financial situation, creating a realistic budget, and exploring retirement savings options, you equip yourself with the knowledge and tools to navigate the complexities of retirement planning. With that knowledge in hand, you can set achievable goals, and adapt to any changes or challenges that may arise along the way. You gain a sense of confidence and control over your retirement journey.

Retirement involves more than just financial planning. It's important to maintain an active and fulfilling lifestyle. Participate in activities that keep you mentally, physically, and socially engaged. Consider exploring volunteer opportunities that align with your interests and values. Join clubs or organizations that cater to your hobbies or passions. Take up new hobbies or pursue educational opportunities. By staying active and engaged during retirement, you can enhance your overall well-being and make the most of your retirement experience.

Life is dynamic, so your retirement plan should be flexible. Regularly review your plans to make sure they match your goals. Keep an eye on your savings and investments, and make changes if necessary. Also, consider any changes in your finances, lifestyle, or unexpected events that could affect your retirement plan. By reviewing and adjusting your plan regularly, you can stay on track for a successful retirement journey.

Life expectancy is longer, so you may have more time to enjoy retirement than your parents did. Make the most of this opportunity by creating a fulfilling post-work life.

By considering these various aspects and engaging in comprehensive retirement planning, you can embark on a fulfilling, secure, and enjoyable retirement journey. This will help you make the most of the most amazing period of your life.

References

Anthony, M. (2008). *The New Retirementality: Planning Your Life and Living Your Dreams... At Any Age You Want.* Wiley.

Birken, E. G. (2014). *The Five Years Before You Retire: Retirement Planning When You Need It the Most.* Adams Media.

Burholt, V., Winter, B., Aartsen, M., Constantinou, C., Dahlberg, L., Feliciano, V., De Jong Gierveld, J., Van Regenmortel, S., Waldegrave, C., & Working Group on Exclusion from Social Relations, part of the COST-financed Research Network 'Reducing Old-Age Exclusion: Collaborations in Research and Policy' (ROSENet). (2019). A Critical Review and Development of a Conceptual Model of Exclusion From Social Relations for Older People. *European Journal of Ageing, 17*(1), 3–19. https://doi.org/10.1007/s10433-019-00506-0

Brumberg, R. (2023). Retirement Is One of Life's Major Transitions—Maintaining Cognitive Health Can Make It Easier. *Forbes.* https://www.forbes.com/health/author/rbrumberg

Blieszner, R., Ogletree, A. M., & Adams, R. G. (2019). Friendship in Later Life: A Research Agenda. *Innovation in Aging*, *3*(1). https://doi.org/10.1093/geroni/igz005

Krantz, M., & Carlson, R. C. (2020). *Retirement Planning for Dummies*. Wiley.

King, D. E., & Xiang, J. (2017). Retirement and Healthy Lifestyle: A National Health and Nutrition Examination Survey (NHANES) data report. *The Journal of the American Board of Family Medicine*, *30(2)*, 213–219. https://doi.org/10.3122/jabfm.2017.02.160244

Larimore, T., Lindauer, M., & Ferri, R. A. (2019). *The Bogleheads' Guide to Retirement Planning*. Wiley.

Moeller, P. (2016). *Get What's Yours for Medicare: Maximize Your Coverage, Minimize Your Costs*. Simon & Schuster.

Moss, W. (2017). *You Can Retire Sooner Than You Think: The 5 Money Secrets of the Happiest Retirees*. McGraw-Hill Education.

National Institute of Diabetes and Digestive and Kidney Diseases. (2019). *Health Tips for Older Adults*. https://www.niddk.nih.gov/health-information/weight-management/healthy-eating-physical-activity-for-life/health-tips-for-older-adults

Pascale, R., Primavera, L. H., & Roach, R. (2012). *The Retirement Maze: What You Should Know Before and After You Retire*. Rowman & Littlefield Publishers.

Ryan, R. (2013). *Retirement Reinvention: Make Your Next Act Your Best Act*. Penguin.

Solin, D. R. (2017). *The Smartest Retirement Book You'll Ever Read: Achieve Your Retirement Dreams—in Any Economy*. Penguin.

Zelinski, E. J. (2016). *How to Retire Happy, Wild, and Free: Retirement Wisdom That You Won't Get from Your Financial Advisor*. Visions International Publishing.

Made in the USA
Middletown, DE
20 December 2023

46403760R00099